Those who are familiar with Sue Eenigenburg's writing will be delighted to learn she has gifted us with another collection of stories. And those who haven't yet discovered her are in for a treat. Sue's conversational style filled with laugh-out-loud anecdotes is present on every page. Mingling Scripture with her extensive global experience, she points followers of Jesus back to the Savior for their source of help and purpose. Her topics are those we all relate to—transition, fear, health, raising children, missing grandchildren, and leaving a legacy. While focused primarily on cross-cultural life, those who haven't lived overseas will also benefit from this daily devotional. Let these real-life testimonies and mini-Bible studies give you the strength you need to face your everyday life.

EVA BURKHOLDER
Member Care Lead, Christar US
Co-author, *Grit to Stay Grace to Go*

Sue is a gifted communicator with breadth of experience and depth of insight! Her godly wisdom is an encouragement to women in all stages of life. She always adds a bit of humor that is both relatable and honest. As a cross-cultural worker myself, a mom of young children, and someone in the midst of many transitions, reading Sue's words acted like a healing balm and always pointed me back to the person and work of Jesus. I'd highly recommend this book for all women in ministry!

LYNNIE GRAY
Cross-cultural worker

Reading Sue's *Bags Packed, Hearts Ready* is like having coffee with a missionary mentor. This book is largely about the transition back "home" at the end of her career, a topic not as written about as often as a missionary's first transition overseas. Her insightful stories are filled with honesty, humor, and spiritual wisdom. Anyone feeling alone in a similar transition will find a friend in this book.

KARLA H.
Cross-cultural worker

Sue Eenigenburg has not disappointed in choosing this needed topic of *Bags Packed, Hearts Ready*, giving us a fresh resource—*especially for her comrades in global ministry*. With her signature humor and ability to tell a story, she gifts us by tethering the truths of her experiences to Scripture. Each vignette welcomes and invites us to relate the topics and truths to our own experiences. Readers are *centered* by her vulnerability and global perspective, encouraging us to *lean into* those promises of God. Because legacy begins when we share our stories, we are inspired to write and share our own. Thank you, Sue.

DORCAS HARBIN
Executive Vice President, One Another Ministries International

Uprooting and rooting again in a foreign land can be isolating. It's a gift when you encounter a sister on the journey who gets the cross-cultural life. Sue is that friend who comes alongside you through her wit and wisdom in the pages of this book to offer her wealth of experiences and the gentle reminder that we all need to hold tight to Jesus through every twist and turn.

Sarah Hilkemann
Program Director, Velvet Ashes

As Sue crosses the ocean for yet another transition, she shares a delightful collection of life stories to mentor her readers through the lens of her experiences in the latter season of cross-cultural ministry. As always, she writes each chapter with creative candor and a wonderful sense of humor followed by three practical questions to help us identify where the Lord might be working in our own lives.

I have witnessed time and again how the Lord has used Sue's teaching and writing to encourage hundreds of women on the field in their spiritual journeys. Praise God that she pressed into her God-given passion to teach God's Word! I pray many women will feel known within the community of global women as they see themselves in her stories!

Lorrie Lindgren
CEO/President, Thrive Ministry

Bags Packed, Hearts Ready is a book that I would recommend, not only for missionaries, but for those who want to understand more of the life of a missionary. Missionaries will read and shake their heads, yes, because they totally understand what's written here. Those who haven't been missionaries will shake their heads in disbelief as they read some of the struggles told about in this book. So, a book for all to read, no matter what place in life you are in.

Beverly Richardson, PhD
A Lodging Place

If you're looking for a book from a great story-telling mentor who's been where you are, you've found it. *Bags Packed, Hearts Ready* is a compilation of stories that will find you nodding your head in recognition as you read them. Each story comes with a companion Scripture, three questions, and a prayer. This book is ideal for those who want to journal responses to the questions, discuss with a friend or spouse, or use for team time. Thank you Sue for sharing your wisdom with us!

Amy Young
Author, *Looming Transitions*
Founder, Global Trellis

Bags Packed, Hearts Ready

Stories of God's Faithfulness in Cross-Cultural Ministry

Sue Eenigenburg

visit us at missionbooks.org

Bags Packed, Hearts Ready: Stories of God's Faithfulness in Cross-Cultural Ministry
© 2024 by Sue Eenigenburg. All Rights Reserved.

No part of this book may be reproduced, stored in a retrieval system, or transmitted in any form or by any means—electronic, mechanical, photocopy, recording, or otherwise—without prior written permission from the publisher, except brief quotations used in connection with reviews. This manuscript may not be entered into AI, even for AI training. For permission, email permissions@wclbooks.com. For corrections, email editor@wclbooks.com.

William Carey Publishing (WCP) publishes resources to shape and advance the missiological conversation in the world. We publish a broad range of thought-provoking books and do not necessarily endorse all opinions set forth here or in works referenced within this book.

The URLs included in this workbook are provided for personal use only and are current as of the date of publication, but the publisher disclaims any obligation to update them after publication.

All Scripture quotations, unless otherwise indicated, are taken from the Holy Bible, New International Version®, NIV®. Copyright ©1973, 1978, 1984, 2011 by Biblica, Inc.™ Used by permission of Zondervan. All rights reserved worldwide. www.zondervan.com. The "NIV" and "New International Version" are trademarks registered in the United States Patent and Trademark Office by Biblica, Inc.™

Scripture quotations marked ESV are taken from the ESV® Bible (The Holy Bible, English Standard Version®), Copyright © 2001 by Crossway, a publishing ministry of Good News Publishers. Used by permission. All rights reserved.

Scripture quotations marked NASB are taken from the NASB® New American Bible®, Copyright © 1960, 1971, 1977, 1995, 2020 by The Lockman Foundation. Used by permission. All rights reserved. lockman.org.

Published by William Carey Publishing
10 W. Dry Creek Cir
Littleton, CO 80120 | www.missionbooks.org

William Carey Publishing is a ministry of Frontier Ventures
Pasadena, CA | www.frontierventures.org

Cover and Interior Designer: Mike Riester

ISBNs: 978-1-64508-598-0 (paperback)
       978-1-64508-599-7 (epub)

Printed Worldwide
28 27 26 25 24   1 2 3 4 5   IN

Library of Congress Control Number: 2024946682

Dedication

To my grandchildren—Sophie, Stacy, Alivia, Dean, Penelope, Hadley, Justin, Natalie, Thomas, Lizzy, Margo, and Nina—who will all have their own "God is faithful" stories to share.

For the LORD is good and his love endures forever;
his faithfulness continues through all generations.
(Psalm 100:5)

Contents

Introduction	ix
1 17 Moves and Counting	1
2 A Regret	4
3 Hiding Weakness Doesn't Make Me Strong	7
4 Big Girls Do Cry	10
5 Dangerous Thinking—"This Is How It Could Be!"	14
6 Comparing Treasures	18
7 Fear-Based Courage	21
8 Faithful Through All Generations	24
9 God Never Sends Us Where He Hasn't Been	27
10 Practicing Gratitude	31
11 How Do We Know When We Are Considered Older?	34
12 Is Wisdom Overrated?	38
13 Hands Off My Alabaster Jar!	41
14 A Walk in the Cemetery	45
15 Living Eulogies	48
16 When It Is OK to Talk to Yourself	52
17 Mopping, Missioning, and Mothering	55
18 What Is Your Name?	59
19 One Foot in the Air	63
20 Bracing	67
21 Therapy	70
22 Selfish Ambition	73
23 Running, Deception, and Spiritual Grit	76
24 Changing Roles and Tangled Emotions	79
25 Informal Mentoring	83
26 Though His Footprints Are Unseen	87
27 The Walking Stick	90
28 Life-Long Faith, Grit, and Grace	93
29 Transition, Grumbling, and Gratitude	96
30 He Who Hesitates Isn't Always Lost	99
31 A Pretzel Is Not a Strawberry and Other Lessons!	102

32	Waiting on the Who, Not the What	105
33	More Than Human Hope	108
34	Sometimes I Miss Me	111
35	Seeking Wisdom	114
36	When God Says You're Old—You Must Be!	117
37	What Would I Tell My Younger Me Starting My First Term Overseas?	120
38	Gideon and "Just One Earring"	123
39	Therefore, We Will Not Fear	126
40	My Whiny Voice Within	129
41	Parenting Seemed Easy, Until I Had Kids!	132
42	Healing Is a Process, Not an Event	135
43	Me and My Frother: A Life Lesson	138
44	Upended by COVID-19 but Not Undone	141
45	Legacy: Earrings and Beyond	145
46	Anxiety About Tomorrow Imprisons Me Today	148
47	Adjusting to a "To-Go Cup" Mindset	151
48	God Is Near and There	154
49	What About Blob?	157
50	Lessons from Blob	160
51	The Panic Button	163
52	From Selfies to Otheries!	166
53	Optimism or Pessimism	169
54	Fishing in Community	172
55	She Kept Pouring	175
56	Evelyn's Legacy of Praying	178
57	Ripples	181
58	An Unforgettable Date	184
59	Uni-Tasking	187
60	Hellos, Goodbyes, and Ugly Cries	191
61	Saying Goodbye as the One Who Stays	194
Acknowledgments		197

Introduction

What is my favorite thing about growing older? Having a longer history of experiencing God's faithfulness. I can look back and see his presence with me in real deserts—and the dry spells where my soul felt like it was in a desert.

When I was younger, I longed for an older person to share their stories with me. I wanted them to bequeath to me gems of wisdom they picked up along the way. Now that I am older, and lots more people are younger than me, I have some stories I would like to share. I've learned helpful tidbits that I wish someone would have shared with me when I was younger.

One older missionary visited me when I was in the throes of raising children and seeking to plant a church. It was hard. She helped me fold laundry and asked me, "What are you afraid of?" I told her, "I am afraid that my underwear will fall off our fifth-floor balcony." She encouraged me and told me if that was one of my biggest fears, I was doing OK.

I worried about the police imprisoning my husband for sharing the gospel. An older couple with much experience said it would be OK. It's hardest the first time but after that it gets easier.

Time and time again, the Lord would send someone my way who understood how I was feeling. They encouraged me that I wasn't alone and that God was watching over me.

It is my prayer that this book will be that kind of encouragement for you. In our thirty-eight years of cross-cultural ministry, I have had ups and downs. Laughter, tears, challenges, and joys. But never once was I alone. Our good shepherd was with me, coming after me when I lost my way and keeping me secure in his green pastures.

May you enjoy these stories. Laugh when you can relate to how funny it is and cry when you have experienced that same sadness. Read the Scripture passages several times. They are short. Respond to the questions. Use the prayer that I wrote as a springboard to speak your own to the Lord.

I am committed to following God until the end of my days. It is my heart's desire to encourage those coming along behind me. The psalmist wrote in Psalm 71:17–18:

Since my youth, God, you have taught me,
> and to this day I declare your marvelous deeds.

Even when I am old and gray,
> do not forsake me, my God,

till I declare your power to the next generation,
> your mighty acts to all who are to come.

I declare to you he will do mighty things in and through you as you follow his call on your life.

1
17 Moves and Counting

Packing again. We plan to be gone for four months. If no one rents our apartment by the time we return, we may move back in! But it doesn't matter because we still must pack and store everything!

Regardless of whether we move back in or have to find a new place, this makes our seventeenth move in forty-five years of marriage. Seven of those have been international. Moving, whether it is country to country or around the block, is hard. It is a lot of packing either way! Sorting through it all and deciding what to keep and what to toss can be stressful and both decisions cause grief.

Years ago, our language school gave us a painting as a thank-you gift. It was a copy of "The Angelus" originally entitled "Prayer for the Potato Crop" by Millet. It portrayed a man and his wife in the field pausing in their work to pray. I loved its beauty and meaning. We had limited space, and the painting wouldn't fit in our luggage. I am thankful it found a good home with new believers in Jesus. But I mourned its loss. Even today, when I remember it, I wish I had it to hang on our wall.

For another move, one of our kids had made a basket in his pottery class at school. Handmade and special, we packed it to take with us. Somehow in the move it broke, and we had to throw it away. It seems silly to be so sad over a broken possession from so many years ago. Yet I still remember my keen disappointment seeing the shattered pieces.

On one of our trips back to the US after our first few terms of overseas ministry, we were at my parents' home. We were looking through things we had stored there. I came upon a big box. Not sure what was in it, I opened it only to find other smaller boxes. Empty boxes. I looked at my dad and asked, "Why would I do this?" He said, "I have no idea." Why I could hang on to a box of empty boxes and not keep more treasured items, I don't know!

With every move, no matter how often I've done it, a sense of instability maneuvers its way into my soul. Moving always involves some uncertainty. Emotions fluctuate. Grieving sometimes and rejoicing sometimes over what was. I seek to dwell in the "what is" world yet wonder about the "what will come." Sometimes I processed emotions and transitions well and other times I didn't. Regardless, it was never easy.

So once again I wrap up my teacups and put away pictures. Boxes are now lined up on shelves. Bubble wrap is in a tidy little pile. Other piles aren't quite so tidy! It won't be long, and we will be transient again. We will travel, share ministry updates, and connect with family and friends. This all adds to my sense of not belonging to any one place or tribe. But, on the other hand, I find out that because of being in God's family, I can belong about anywhere! My tribe is large and spread out around the world!

As we sort, pack, and travel, rumblings reverberate in my soul: "You are rootless—insecure, unsettled, adrift." These are lies. The truth is that by God's grace I have the certain assurance that I am securely rooted in Jesus. Wherever I go. Whether I am in a home or traveling without one. Whether I have my things with me or not. Whether I even have things or not. I don't find my refuge and strength in where I am or what I own. My security comes from God, knowing I belong to him.

I am grateful for the privilege to do what we do and to serve where we are. I appreciate yet another opportunity to realize anew the certainty of my calling to Jesus. Wherever I go and wherever I live in this uncertain world, there remains the certainty that I am his and he is mine.

Scripture

> See what great love the Father has lavished on us, that we should be called children of God! And that is what we are! The reason the world does not know us is that it did not know him. Dear friends, now we are children of God, and what we will be has not yet been made known. But we know that when Christ appears, we shall be like him, for we shall see him as he is. (1 John 3:1–2)

Questions

1. What emotions does "move" stir in your soul?

2. What losses have you grieved in your moves?

3. How does God's calling and presence soothe your heart?

Prayer

I am so grateful that I am your daughter. Nothing can sway your love for me. My roots are deep, and I can't be shaken loose. Sometimes, I feel muddled in this world with different homes and cultures speaking into my life. I try to figure out how to live well wherever I am and at times it is so hard to adapt because I am uncomfortable. Keep me close to you and help me remember my forever home is with you. Amen.

2
A Regret

In thinking of our early years in cross-cultural ministry, I have a regret. Actually, I have more than one, but this is one I've been pondering.

The culture where our team ministered was resistant to the gospel. At various times there were crackdowns on those who shared Jesus Christ's gift of salvation with people. If there was a complaint against someone, or if someone was too bold or gave literature to an informant, that person might be in trouble. Police could take him in for questioning. He could be released, imprisoned, or deported. We saw all three things take place among people we knew. I can't think of any western minister who was severely tortured or martyred. I do know of national believers who were, and I felt powerless to help them.

The government in that country used fear as a weapon to effectively keep people in line. Secret police tracked what was going on in the country. They routinely visited churches. When small groups of believers met together, some were enticed or coerced by authorities to provide information on friends. There was always the tension of seeking to be wise and yet bold when sharing the gospel.

For someone who tends to be timid and more compliant—like me—the temptation to give into fear when under strain can feel overwhelming. I don't like getting into trouble, and I don't like causing other people trouble. My regret is that I let fear become a factor in my own life more often than I care to admit. As a result of that fear, guilt entered the picture when I shared the gospel. This is not good for a person called to ministry!

I remember one time in particular feeling a heavy burden of guilt after sharing the story of Jesus with my national friend. At first, she seemed excited about Jesus and his love for her, but then as she thought about consequences of choosing to believe in him her eyes dimmed.

She asked me, "Do you know what would happen to me if I believed the gospel?" I did know. She could lose her home, her husband, her children, and her life. All that she loved could be stripped away from her for trusting in Jesus. I felt like I was inviting her to a life of misery and not to God's wonderful plan for her life. In my sadness I turned to God's Word and read Hebrews 10:32–39 soon after that encounter:

> Remember those earlier days after you had received the light, when you endured in a great conflict full of suffering. Sometimes you were publicly exposed to insult and persecution; at other times you stood side by side with those who were so treated. You suffered along with those in prison and joyfully accepted the confiscation of your property, because you knew that you yourselves had better and lasting possessions. So do not throw away your confidence; it will be richly rewarded.
>
> You need to persevere so that when you have done the will of God, you will receive what he has promised. For,
>
> > "In just a little while,
> >   he who is coming will come,
> >   and will not delay."
>
> And,
>
> > "But my righteous one will live by faith.
> >   And I take no pleasure
> >   in the one who shrinks back."
>
> But we do not belong to those who shrink back and are destroyed, but to those who have faith and are saved.

I should not be asking her to lose something that I am not also prepared to lose. Knowing and following Jesus in this life is not always easy. However, he has promised not only to never leave us, but to give peace and joy through whatever suffering we encounter in this world. He also promises us an eternal home in heaven with him. I had to keep in mind what we gain in eternity, not focus on what we could lose temporarily. God's Word emboldened me to keep sharing the gospel. By faith overcoming fear, I could determine not to let the momentary overtake the eternal. This life is fleeting; the life to come is everlasting.

Scripture

Then Jesus said to his disciples, "Whoever wants to be my disciple must deny themselves and take up their cross and follow me. For whoever wants to save their life will lose it, but whoever loses their life for me will find it. What good will it be for someone to gain the whole world, yet forfeit their soul? Or what can anyone give in exchange for their soul?"

(Matt 16:24–26)

Questions

1. How has fear influenced your life and witness?

2. What is one of your regrets?

3. How could keeping your focus on eternity change your perspective?

Prayer

Father, please continue to help me stand firm by faith and not shrink back. May I consistently choose loving Jesus over loving temporary possessions and momentary safety. May I incessantly and fearlessly love others and point them to Jesus. He is our only eternal hope amid a fleeting world. Amen.

3
Hiding Weakness Doesn't Make Me Strong

I am known for having a terrible sense of direction. I used to try and hide it, but it really is impossible to hide when you must always ask which way to turn. It can be embarrassing. Google maps has helped quite a bit, but sometimes even Google can't help me.

We were visiting family. Their house is a sprawling ranch, and I was unfamiliar with its layout. We spent the night in the guest room. I slept later than my husband Don, so he had already left the room. When it was time for breakfast, I opened our bedroom door to the long hallway. We were in the middle room and there were two closed doors on either end. I didn't know which way to go. One room led to breakfast. The other room was our hosts' bedroom. I didn't want to open the wrong door.

I assumed that when Don noticed that I was not there when breakfast started, he would come let me know it was ready and lead the way. So, I waited.

It was now past time for breakfast. He didn't come. I looked in the hallway again. Nothing had changed. I felt so silly. They were probably waiting for me before they started breakfast and thought I was running late. Nope. I was just stuck because I didn't want to open the wrong door.

Brilliance struck. I will text Don to find out. So I did. "Hey, which way do I go down the hall? Doors are closed at both ends and I can't remember."

I waited. He didn't respond. Ugh.

I hated what I was going to have to do next. I would have to call him. Now my brother and sister-in-law would be more aware of my weakness. I get lost even in houses. How embarrassing! But it would be more so if I never came out of the room!

I'm sure it surprised Don that it was me on the phone. I explained to him my situation and to his credit he wasn't laughing too hard. He came to help and opened the right door. I joined them for breakfast.

They were very gracious. No one laughed at me. I still felt foolish. I hate this weakness that is hard to hide. Normally I can laugh about it and tell people upfront not to ask me for directions. But when I must ask for help for what is easy for others, I detest this weakness more. It makes me feel stupid. Who else would get lost in a house? Who else is too timid to knock on a door to find out if it is the right one? Who else must call their husband to ask for directions to breakfast when they are in the same house?

Asking for help reveals my weaknesses to others. I want to be strong and self-sufficient, or at least appear to be. Asking for help highlights that I am not always able. My heart can be proud. Asking for help requires humility.

Independence is admirable in my western culture. Philippians 4:13 was a memory verse from my teen years. "I can do all this through him who gives me strength." It is a good verse. A true verse. But it doesn't mean I never need other people. It doesn't mean that all my weaknesses disappear. It means that with Jesus I can do what he calls me to do in the strength he provides.

He didn't make me or call me to be good with directions. We all have strengths. We all have weaknesses. We need each other. That is why God put us in the body of Christ. Under his direction, we each serve as he has gifted.

I didn't memorize Philippians 4:14 until a few years ago: "Yet it was good of you to share in my troubles." When we have troubles, weaknesses, or challenges, people come alongside us and help. Sometimes people see we need help and offer it. Other times we can ask. It doesn't mean that Christ isn't giving us strength. It means that he is using others to help us along. This is a wonderful testimony to loving one another.

Pride causes me to fear others' opinions. If they see my weaknesses, they will know I am not always strong. I don't always have my act together. The thing is, we should all know that about each other anyway. We are weak. Pride makes us want to pretend we are strong so that others will be impressed with us.

Humility helps us acknowledge that we need help so that Jesus is honored when he gives us strength. When others step in to share in my troubles and help me, it is a testimony to the love we have for one another because of Jesus and his love for us.

For the glory of God. Not us.

Scripture

But he said to me, "My grace is sufficient for you, for my power is made perfect in weakness." Therefore I will boast all the more gladly about my weaknesses, so that Christ's power may rest on me. That is why, for Christ's sake, I delight in weaknesses, in insults, in hardships, in persecutions, in difficulties. For when I am weak, then I am strong. (2 Cor 12:9–10)

Questions

1. What weaknesses most embarrass you?

2. How has hiding weaknesses hindered your reliance on God?

3. How can you develop humility?

Prayer

I'm so thankful you use weak people. You already know all my weaknesses. I might hide them from people, but you know. Help me recognize that living in my own strength and seeking to rely on myself limits how I can serve you. May I seek to be filled with your Spirit and live by your grace and power. Amen.

4
Big Girls Do Cry

I spent a week in the US helping to care for my mom. She had been sick, and I was happy to be able to fly home to help her. When I was with my mom she would say, "I'm so sorry. I'm causing so much trouble." I would respond, "No mom, this is a delight for me to be here and help take care of you. I love you." Thankful that my mom was feeling better, I began my way back home.

I was walking through the airport corridor when my shoe caught on the smooth floor causing my feet to stop. But my body kept going. Struggling to recapture my balance, I failed. Falling on the hard floor, I lost one shoe in the process and struggled to stand up. Shaken, but with the help of passersby, I got my shoe back on and stood. I limped to a nearby chair to sit down and recover. Sitting down was easy, but I was in pain and could barely stand.

I saw an airport information desk nearby and hobbled over to ask for help. A cart transported me to my departing gate. As I sat with two hours left until boarding time, my knee pain increased. My right arm was hurting. My plan was to get on the plane and get home as quickly as possible, but after texting with my husband and daughter, we decided that was not a good idea. We thought it best to seek medical treatment before taking the eight-hour flight with a twelve-hour layover on my way home.

A customer service representative arranged for a cart to drive me to the area where I could wait for my daughter to pick me up. The cart dropped me off at the beginning of a long hallway. The driver told me to walk straight ahead, go down the escalator, and I would find the area to wait for my daughter.

I couldn't believe I was going to have to walk all that way. I saw an empty wheelchair, so I asked her if I could have it. She asked if I had someone to push it. Hmm. No, I didn't. She directed me again to walk down the corridor, go down the escalator and there I would find a wheelchair and people to help. Leaning into the wall for support, I began limping slowly, hoping to make it to my destination. (My husband asks me to mention at this part in the story why I didn't insist on more help. I honestly didn't think of it. I am not the most assertive person in the world and if she told me to walk, walk I would.)

Forging ahead, I made it to the escalator and on the ground floor I saw a bathroom to the left. I made a quick detour and entered the stall. Closed off from the world, I felt the pain and despair wash over me. At the end of my emotional and physical strength, I was on the verge of sobbing when I heard the song "Big Girls Don't Cry" playing over the sound system. I had to laugh at the timing, though my circumstances weren't funny.

I eventually found the wheelchair station and waited for my daughter to pick me up. While waiting, I thought about that song. I used to think it was fun, but I never thought about how much of a lie it is. Big girls *do* cry. And it's OK. When we are sad. When we are in pain or see others suffering. When we watch sad movies. Or even when we fall, hurt ourselves, and must keep walking. It is OK to cry.

My daughter arranged with her work and family to come pick me up. She took me to an urgent care facility where we discovered I had a fractured kneecap and a fractured arm bone.

My daughter took me home with her to spend the night. She had to help me in and out of the car. She made the sofa into a bed for me. She gave me medicine, lent me pajamas, and washed my clothes so I could travel the next day with a fresh start. I remember saying to her, "I'm so sorry. I'm so much trouble." That sounded vaguely familiar to me. And then I remembered where I heard it as she replied with similar words I had used with my mom, "It's OK. I'm glad I'm here to help." Which made me cry thankful tears. She was happy to help me as I had been happy to help my mom. I cried as I reflected on God's care for me on my journey through strangers, friends, and family. We all help each other. I also cried tears of pain. My body hurt.

Big girls do cry. And in our tears, we are comforted. Sometimes God alone soothes our souls. Other times, he uses family and friends to offer solace. The Lord doesn't see our tears as a sign of weakness, but as an invitation for his comfort. The psalmist reminds us, "The LORD is close to the brokenhearted and saves those who are crushed in spirit" (Ps 34:18).

Even as I type these words, I've heard my mom is back in the hospital facing severe medical challenges and I weep. I'm a big girl who cries and am welcomed onto her heavenly father's lap to be held by his everlasting arms.

You are welcome to join me.

Scripture

When Mary reached the place where Jesus was and saw him, she fell at his feet and said, "Lord, if you had been here, my brother would not have died."

When Jesus saw her weeping, and the Jews who had come along with her also weeping, he was deeply moved in spirit and troubled. "Where have you laid him?" he asked.

"Come and see, Lord," they replied.

Jesus wept.

Then the Jews said, "See how he loved him!" (John 11:32–36)

Questions

1. What are some benefits of crying?

2. Describe a time you felt comforted by another person.

3. How have you experienced God's comfort recently?

Prayer

You know the pain in my heart. You see my sorrow like no one else. You know when despair begins to fill my heart and I forget about hope. I am never alone in my sadness. You are always with me. My tears won't drive you away. You are near. Thank you for knowing me and giving me a Comforter who will never leave. Amen.

5
Dangerous Thinking—"This Is How It Could Be!"

I was visiting my daughter to help her after my granddaughter, Margo, was born. There were special bonding moments with her and practical opportunities to help my daughter as she adjusted to being a mother of two. I cooked and cleaned, did laundry, and swept floors—all the things that are so much more fun when you do it for people you love and not just for yourself!

While there, another granddaughter became ill and had to go to the emergency room. I was driving to be with my daughter-in-law as she sat with her sick daughter and on the way to the hospital I was thinking, "This is how it could be!" I could live in America and be here all the time when things like this happen. I would be a help to these young families. I could have daily contact with these six precious little ones. And from that springboard were other perceived benefits—I could go to a church where people know me. I could find things easily at the grocery store. I would be in my more comfortable home culture. I found myself longing for the "this is how it could be life."

The problem with longing for the "this is how it could be life" is that as soon as we try to live that way, make the necessary changes, and think we might have found it, circumstances change. People move. Kids grow up. Cultures evolve. Stores close. Pastors leave. And we end up living a new reality that also loses its appeal and yet again something happens that seems magical, special, or simply more convenient, and we think, "This is how it could be!" and we start longing for a different type of life again.

The "this is how it could be life" is usually illusive. Sometimes it is a fantasy. Other times it is a lie that Satan uses to deceive our hearts and grow discontentment in the very fibers of our souls.

The "what is" life is constantly changing—especially as cross-cultural workers with so many hellos and goodbyes. We meet teammates and network with other organizations. Government officials deny visas; politics change; wars simmer; coups erupt. In unstable situations like these we are tempted to yearn for the "this is how it could be life"—longing for our home countries where everything we remember is wonderful, easy, and good. This is known as selective memory!

The only sure foundation on which to live out life is the "what will be world" which is ordained by God. The only certainty in life is that the plan of God cannot and will not be thwarted.

Based on what will be, how do I live my life today? What is God's calling? Yes, it is to be a wife, mother, and grandmother in his kingdom. These are roles I relish, and I am thankful for opportunities to live out these ways to love, serve, and influence family whether I am near or far.

He has also called me to use my gifts for the kingdom outside of my home; to follow him no matter what the cost. Sometimes this means that I am called to live away from family. Other times this could mean I live near them. What it always means is that primarily I seek to do the will of God and follow where he leads.

As I was packing to fly back to Europe, I didn't want to leave. I had thoroughly enjoyed several wonderful weeks of family time. I had sleepovers, tea parties, walks to the park, play time, and special late-night dates with baby Margo. I had the chance to reconnect with my kids, and I hated to say goodbye.

My body got on the plane. My heart arrived about one week later.

My heart arrived about the time I realized my longing to live in a "this is how it could be world" was unrealistic and unobtainable. I recognized that even if we moved back to America, I wouldn't necessarily live in the same state where I visited; that I couldn't recreate the same opportunities or permanently live with my daughter in a guest room. That wouldn't be good for them or me.

Rather than long for a deceptive dream I can choose to be thankful for the reality I experience. I can enjoy the memories of snuggling babies, giggling toddlers, and engaging children. I can be grateful for the privilege of being in the right place at the right time to be of help to my kids. I can still take advantage of technology to communicate and keep relationships growing.

In taking the needed time to reflect on God's calling and what that looks like in my life, I realized anew that I am honored to serve Jesus with my husband in this small corner of the world. I recollected that our time on earth is limited, and we must do all we can to see our family members *and* least-reached peoples of the world hear about the one and only Savior of the world.

I must let the truth of what will be influence how I live today and how I handle the "this is how it could be" in my imagination.

Scripture

Anyone who loves their father or mother more than me is not worthy of me; anyone who loves their son or daughter more than me is not worthy of me. Whoever does not take up their cross and follow me is not worthy of me. Whoever finds their life will lose it, and whoever loses their life for my sake will find it. (Matt 10:37–39)

Questions

1. What is your ideal image of a "this is how it could be life"?

2. What role does gratitude play when living where God has you?

3. How can you say goodbyes well?

Prayer

Being in your family, living out my calling, following you step by step are all amazing blessings. Sometimes it is hard. Other times I can't imagine living any other way. May I always seek to do your will and love you most. Amen.

6
Comparing Treasures

The wise men had treasures to present to Jesus:

> After they had heard the king, they went on their way, and the star they had seen when it rose went ahead of them until it stopped over the place where the child was. When they saw the star, they were overjoyed. On coming to the house, they saw the child with his mother Mary, and they bowed down and worshiped him. Then they opened their treasures and presented him with gifts of gold, frankincense, and myrrh. (Matt 2:9–11)

Their gifts were impressive and expensive. Considering what I bring to Jesus, I see nothing as amazing as theirs. And, when I compare the gifts that I give with what I see other global workers offering, I feel deficient. I want to bring something remarkable to Jesus, but even my best pales when I compare it to what others bring.

Comparisons are dangerous. All the gifts we have are from God. He chooses what to give us. Thinking our gifts aren't adequate is an insult to the Giver of all gifts. Also, our focus switches from his pleasure as we receive our gifts, to ourselves and what we want.

It isn't our perceived value of a gift that makes it important. Everything we have to give comes from the God we are giving it to! God chooses to use whatever we bring to him however he wants.

Any gift we offer to God, when presented by faith, honors him.

I remember David's sling, the widow's mite, and the little boy's lunch.

When facing a giant, David had no sword, no armor. He had no weapon that people thought would be appropriate to fight a big battle. Yet, he took what he had—five stones and a sling. Taking aim with what he had, the giant fell. It wasn't the size of the weapon but our big God who used a small stone to do the impossible.

Jesus said of the widow's mite that she gave more than the rich because she gave out of her poverty. She gave all that she had. In the world's eyes, her few cents were worthless. In God's eyes, her gift was pleasing.

When all the people were hungry and there was only a little boy's lunch, the disciples knew it wasn't enough. There were thousands of people. And yet, as Jesus gave thanks and blessed it, the boy's few fish and loaves of bread fed them all. It wasn't that the boy gave a lot; it was God who made the little abundant.

When I open my treasures, they are all gifts that God gave me so that I can give them back to him with thanksgiving and pleasure. In the world's eyes, and even my own, they aren't much. Yet, God specializes in using insignificant things to achieve his big purposes.

When we open our treasures and present our gifts to God, he is pleased to receive them and has plans to use them. Our eyes shouldn't be on the gifts, but on God. God isn't looking at how our gifts compare with what others give, but on our hearts as we present them to him.

I am sure the wise men's focus was not on what each other brought. They were gazing at the babe in the manger, God's gift to save the world.

Thanks be to God for his indescribable gift! (2 Cor 9:15)

Scripture

> There are different kinds of gifts, but the same Spirit distributes them. There are different kinds of service, but the same Lord. There are different kinds of working, but in all of them and in everyone it is the same God at work. (1 Cor 12:4–6)

Questions

1. What spiritual gifts do you wish you had?

2. How do comparisons harm relationships in the body of Christ?

3. Who decides what gifts to give to whom? How would knowing this affect envy?

Prayer

God, I am sorry for complaining about gifts and wishing I had what others have. My gifts aren't for my significance or to prove my value to the kingdom. They are given to be used by you for your glory. Forgive me when I envy. Thank you for the gifts you've given to me. I give them back to you with joy and contentment, knowing your purposes are good. Amen.

7
Fear-Based Courage

I love reading true stories about courageous people. I try to put myself in their shoes and wonder if I could ever do what they did. I have my doubts, but by God's grace and power there is at least a possibility! Whereas in my own strength, it would be a definite no.

In Scripture, I read about people who faced formidable circumstances, and their courage remained undaunted. The Hebrew midwives in the land of Egypt disobeyed Pharaoh because they feared God more than him. We read in Exodus 1:15–17:

> The king of Egypt said to the Hebrew midwives, whose names were Shiphrah and Puah, "When you are helping the Hebrew women during childbirth on the delivery stool, if you see that the baby is a boy, kill him; but if it is a girl, let her live." The midwives, however, feared God and did not do what the king of Egypt had told them to do; they let the boys live.

Picture with me others in the Bible who didn't know the end of their stories. Daniel faced lions. Esther went in to see the king knowing she might die. Rahab sheltered the spies. David fought Goliath. Shadrach, Meshach, and Abednego encountered a burning furnace. These young men said to King Nebuchadnezzar in Daniel 3:16b–18:

> "We do not need to defend ourselves before you in this matter. If we are thrown into the blazing furnace, the God we serve is able to deliver us from it, and he will deliver us from Your Majesty's hand. But even if he does not, we want you to know, Your Majesty, that we will not serve your gods or worship the image of gold you have set up."

They knew God was all powerful and they knew what he *could* do. They weren't sure what he *would* do, but they trusted him no matter the outcome.

We know God too. We have the opportunity each day to trust him. Knowing I am not a courageous person, I used to think that my timidity made me unqualified to serve God. He would be looking for brave people, strong ones who fear nothing. Come to find out, when we are afraid and realize our need for God, he gives the strength we need. As a result, he receives the glory! Weakness and fear remind us that we need God, and we rely on him.

God's grace has helped me stay when I wanted to run to safety. I remember heart-hammering fear and recurring uncertainty. I wanted to escape the stress. I needed God. He met me where I was. He gave me courage to stand firm when all I wanted to do was flee.

Circumstances do not determine whether we are courageous or not. What we face does not have the power to dispel courage. God gives courage to us and uses circumstances to display that strength comes from him.

In my uncertainty, he was my certainty. In my weakness, he was my strength. Maybe the fear won't ever totally go away, but it doesn't have to win. God gives victory over fear.

Scripture

> The LORD is my light and my salvation—
>   whom shall I fear?
> The LORD is the stronghold of my life—
>   of whom shall I be afraid?
> When the wicked advance against me
>   to devour me,
> it is my enemies and my foes
>   who will stumble and fall.
> Though an army besiege me,
>   my heart will not fear;
> though war break out against me,
>   even then I will be confident.
>
> (Ps 27:1–3)

Questions

1. How has giving in to fear affected your life?

2. What do you need to step out in faith?

3. How have you seen God's faithfulness when you were at your weakest?

Prayer

Father, you see my heart. You know my fears. You are aware of how hard it is when I am feeling weak to step out in faith. My natural inclination is to cower, to shrink back. Your Holy Spirit is able to overcome my fallen nature and sets me free. Thank you for being the stronghold of my life. No matter what is happening all around me I can be confident in you. Amen.

8
Faithful Through All Generations

**For the LORD is good and his love endures forever;
his faithfulness continues through all generations.**
(Ps 100:5)

When my kids were little, I did my best to watch over them, care for them, and help them with challenges. Praying for them was intentional and frequent. This is all a part of what moms and dads do for their children. When possible, I tried to make life easier for them. I sought to meet their needs and did my best to make our home a haven amid cultural challenges at home and abroad. If I saw anything that might hurt them, I did my best to prepare them to face it or protect them from it. I didn't do it perfectly, but I tried hard.

Now that they are adults with families of their own, I find myself wishing I could still do what I attempted then. I want to protect and shield them from life's hardships but am unable to do so. They face many challenges in this ever-changing world that are beyond my capability and control. Even if I think of ways that I could be hands-on help, I am living on a different continent.

As I think about the trials they face and pray for them, I find myself feeling helpless as I compare all my heart *wants* to do for them with what I *can* do. It seemed easier to be of help when they were young. I had more control—or at least the illusion of it.

And then I remember the trials Don and I faced when we were their age. We were trying to survive cultural, spiritual, physical, and emotional hardships. Running away from home seemed appealing to me when I felt overwhelmed with stress. Doubts about my ability as a wife/mother/cross-cultural worker plagued me as I balanced roles. It was often unclear to me what was the best thing to do. I remember wondering where God was when I felt alone. Facing health challenges and fears of what the future might hold alarmed my soul. In trying to learn a foreign language I sometimes felt like an idiot. Wanting to be strong, I encountered weakness. Yet, in every situation, God met me where I was.

By his power, he rescued me. In his kindness, he gave me hope. Out of his mercy, he comforted me. God strengthened my soul. He secured me in his everlasting arms moment by moment, day after day, year after year. I am so grateful to this God of ours: the eternal, unchanging creator, redeemer, and sustainer of all.

As I meditate on who he is and remember his faithfulness, I know he will help my children with whatever they may face in this troubled world. I remember afresh his promise of faithfulness that continues through all generations. He was there for the biblical heroes like Abraham, Ruth, Mary, and Paul. He was there for our parents and grandparents. He is here for my husband and me. He will be there for my kids. He will be there for our grandchildren and all that they encounter. He will be there for their children and their grandchildren and theirs. His faithfulness is certain and eternal.

In the middle of feeling weak and ill equipped, God reminds me of his faithfulness. His faithfulness doesn't change; it is constant through the ages. Remembering who God is gives me hope for present and future generations. He will see all of us through the challenges we are experiencing now and the ones yet to come.

Each day may God open our eyes anew to his faithfulness of old.

Scripture

> **Your word, LORD, is eternal;**
> **it stands firm in the heavens.**
> **Your faithfulness continues through all generations;**
> **you established the earth, and it endures.**
> **Your laws endure to this day,**
> **for all things serve you.**
>
> (Ps 119:89–91)

Questions

1. How do you see God's faithfulness exhibited in previous generations?

2. What fears do you battle for the upcoming generation?

3. What does God's faithfulness mean to you?

Prayer

There is never a time you are absent. Nothing is outside of your control. You are as sovereign now as you were before creation. Your promises are ever true. When I start to worry and am tempted to fear for my children and grandchildren, prompt me to remember your faithfulness shown throughout Scripture and my own life. May I point them to you and remind them of your steadfast faithfulness. Amen.

9
God Never Sends Us Where He Hasn't Been

When Deborah told Barak to go into battle, she pointed out this truth to encourage him: "Has not the LORD gone ahead of you?" (Judg 4:14). God never sends us where he hasn't been. This is a very comforting Scripture verse to me.

As I already shared, I have no sense of direction. I lose my way frequently. Knowing someone knows, that someone has gone ahead of me, is encouraging and motivates me to go. When I am driving, if I have Google maps I can go anywhere, because Google knows what is ahead and it rarely leads me astray.

And God knows more than Google! In life when I am not sure where I am going, not confident of what is ahead, just knowing that God knows and has gone before me makes me braver. God is never surprised. He never throws up his hands and says, "I hadn't thought of that." No, God always knows. He's not limited by time or space. Humans don't know. We can't see into the future.

About three hours after teaching on not having to fear the future because God goes ahead of us, we heard from our landlady. She said she needed her apartment back and we would need to move. She was truly kind giving us three months' notice, but with our upcoming activities and travel schedule we weren't sure we could find a place that soon.

I'm so glad I had just taught this truth so that it was fresh in my mind. God was giving me a chance to practice what I had taught others. He knew about our need for a new flat long before we did. God always goes ahead of us. He knows the future.

Being reassured that God goes ahead of us, we started looking. We tried setting up appointments to see places, but most realtors didn't call us back. A few offered to show us apartments that we didn't want to see. We saw several apartments that didn't quite measure up to the pictures we had seen on-line. We kept looking.

Panic!

I grew discouraged when we didn't see something we liked or when the realtor cancelled an appointment. But I remembered that God knows the future. Tomorrow belongs to him. Today I have a home. By God's grace I would manage today and though I was preparing for tomorrow, I didn't have to borrow tomorrow's problems for today.

None of us know what tomorrow holds. It can look scary. We may be facing a diagnosis or loss of a job or a need to move. Or maybe we think we know exactly what will happen and with confidence in ourselves we step forward. Sometimes things work out like we imagine. Other times they don't. We can't even be sure we have tomorrow.

God has already been there.

He knows.

We found an apartment in record time. This was also when I received the news about my mom's illness and when I fell in the airport. Again, I thought back to what I had recently taught. God knew what was coming my way. The following month my mom passed away. As I headed home for her funeral, I was again reminded of God knowing how all this would transpire and that he was with me each step of the way.

Through months of painful rehab and grieving the loss of my mom, the truth that God had already gone ahead of me kept me focused on him. God in his sovereignty knew what I would need to know to walk into my future. It was no accident that I taught on how God going ahead of us gives us courage. He knows what we don't know; he has been where we haven't been; he sees what we do not see. There are no mysteries, no surprises for God.

I'm glad he leads me into a future he knows. May I trust him as I follow him into tomorrow.

Scripture

So do not worry, saying, "What shall we eat?" or "What shall we drink?" or "What shall we wear?" For the pagans run after all these things, and your heavenly Father knows that you need them. But seek first his kingdom and his righteousness, and all these things will be given to you as well. Therefore do not worry about tomorrow, for tomorrow will worry about itself. Each day has enough trouble of its own. (Matt 6:31–34)

Questions

1. How have you seen God prepare you for an unexpected event?

2. How does knowing that God goes ahead of you give you courage?

3. What fears about tomorrow do you need to give to God today?

Prayer

I praise you that you know everything. You've never experienced mystery or confusion. You always know the future. I don't. I confess that I hate surprises and sometimes I find it hard not to worry. When my kids were little, I remember reading to them a story about a worried sparrow—how much I related to that little bird. Even as an adult! But you care for the sparrow, and you care for me. Today. Tomorrow. Forever. I am blessed. Amen.

10
Practicing Gratitude

It's hard to stop the countdown! Recently, I had only four days for a family visit. Three. Two. One. Then it is leaving and the sadness that entails. This can taint the whole visit as we prepare for the goodbye without fully being present and enjoying the time we have.

During this past visit home, I more intentionally practiced being thankful for the time we had. When I started to think I have only four days left, I would pray, "Thank you for these four days!"

I realized that it wasn't just this way with family but with anything I enjoyed. When I get a bag of Reese's cups, I try to ration them out to make them last. "Only one more left!" comes more easily to my mind than, "Thank you for this Reese's cup." What I enjoy becomes the focus rather than the pleasure of experiencing it.

When it is something that I don't enjoy, there is also a countdown. As I write this, I'm sick with a respiratory infection. My focus is, "How long will this last?" I'm counting down the days until I am feeling better. I am trying to practice gratitude when it is really the farthest thing from my mind. But I am looking to God and saying:

Thank you for medicine.

Thank you for a doctor nearby.

Thank you for making our bodies capable of fighting off germs.

Thank you that I can rest and know that you are with me all the time.

There's something about gratitude that lightens my soul and lifts my burdens. In gratitude, I recognize God as the giver of good things to enjoy. When I'm thankful in challenges, I focus on God being present with me at work for my good and his glory. But too often I feel more like the nine ungrateful lepers that Jesus healed than the one who returned to thank him. The others were so excited about their healing that they forgot who healed them (Luke 17:11–19).

Ingratitude inspires selfishness because I become my focus. Selfishness evolves into being unkind to others because I am consumed with my own needs while others' needs fade into oblivion.

Gratitude, on the other hand, inspires generosity. Recognizing God as the ultimate giver and thanking him makes me more aware of all that I have from him. So much, that I want to give to others. Generosity motivates kindness from others to others.

One small "thank you" changes my attitude. Gratitude changes my heart.

Scripture

> Let the peace of Christ rule in your hearts, since as members of one body you were called to peace. And be thankful. Let the message of Christ dwell among you richly as you teach and admonish one another with all wisdom through psalms, hymns, and songs from the Spirit, singing to God with gratitude in your hearts. And whatever you do, whether in word or deed, do it all in the name of the Lord Jesus, giving thanks to God the Father through him. (Col 3:15–17)

Questions

1. When is being thankful difficult for you?

2. What are the characteristics of a grateful person's heart?

3. How can you develop a thankful heart?

Prayer

I tend to complain. My soul is selfish, and I realize I think more of my comfort than I do of your purposes for me. You are the giver of all good gifts. You are at work in me through joys and challenges. I have all I need in you. Forgive me when I forget that and may I be quick to respond to your Spirit's prompting to be grateful. Thank you. Amen.

11
How Do We Know When We Are Considered Older?

There are a few subtle signs that may give us a hint we are getting close to old age.

- People talk about events in history that happened when you were alive. They seem more recent occurrences to you since you remember them.
- People come up to you (without looking around) hoping to talk with an older person.
- You automatically get a senior discount.
- Younger people (of whom there are more and more) refer to you as ma'am or Mrs. and not by your first name.
- Many people don't understand references to your old favorite shows.
- Age spots pop out on your hands.
- Remembering why you went into a certain room isn't always clear.
- Recalling names, dates and events can be a group effort.

I always knew, though, that the real test for being officially older is when you have wrinkled elbows. For many years, my elbows weren't wrinkled. There was no sagging. And I checked regularly! I always left the mirror quite satisfied that I wasn't old.

Well, I am older. My elbows have wrinkles.

My oldest two kids are in their forties. My younger two aren't far behind. No one says I look too young to be a grandma anymore. Yep, saggy elbows equals being old. I should suggest a memory verse for my kids: "… and do not despise your mother when she is old" (Prov 23:22b).

I firmly believe (when body parts sag, I try to be firm however I can be!) that with age, comes not only wisdom but responsibility. I see this responsibility as two-fold.

One, I have the responsibility and privilege to invest in the next generation. I am so grateful for all I learned from mentors and older friends. I watched them, asked questions, learned from what they said and did. Now I want to be available to others. My heart must be open, ready to share what God has taught me through failure and successes, sorrows and joys. I must be intentional to share the promises from God's word that have been meaningful. I rehearse the principles of living and serving that have proven helpful. I have done well sometimes. I have messed up sometimes. God has been with me each step of the way.

Two, I have the responsibility and privilege to learn from the next generation. I am grateful for the humility of my mentors and older friends who welcomed my contributions. They invited input, asked me about what I was learning, listened to me. They gave me room to grow and didn't stifle my enthusiasm. I want to hear what God is doing in the lives of my young friends. I love seeing how God is at work in and through them. I am eager to benefit from their expertise and wisdom. They may mess up. They will do good. God is with them each step of the way.

Growing older is a gift from God. Backs may ache. Joints can be stiff. Elbows might sag. My grandma used to say, "Getting older isn't for wimps!" But each day is a gift, and I don't want to squander what God has richly given. I am ready to invest in others and I anticipate their involvement in my life.

Our lives will enrich each other's. But some of us will still have saggy elbows.

Scripture

My mouth will tell of your righteous deeds,
    of your saving acts all day long—
    though I know not how to relate them all.
I will come and proclaim your mighty acts, Sovereign LORD;
    I will proclaim your righteous deeds, yours alone.
Since my youth, God, you have taught me,
    and to this day I declare your marvelous deeds.
Even when I am old and gray,
    do not forsake me, my God,
till I declare your power to the next generation,
    your mighty acts to all who are to come. (Ps 71:15–18)

Questions

1. How can multi-generational teams be a blessing to each other?

2. What is one way you can invest in a person younger than you?

3. What is one thing you would like to learn from a person younger than you?

Prayer

Thank you for the gift of life. Thank you for the privilege of seeing a new generation come to know and serve you. Thank you for a growing history of experiencing your faithfulness. It is an honor to share your faithfulness to me with others. I have limited energy, and I don't know how much longer I have to live for you here. May I be wise and finish well to honor you now and into eternity. Amen.

12
Is Wisdom Overrated?

I've always admired Solomon. When God told him to ask for whatever he wanted Solomon chose wisdom. He could have asked for long life or wealth, but he didn't. He knew what he needed to rule well; he desired wisdom. God was pleased with his request and in God's kindness and providence, he added riches and honor to the wisdom for Solomon.

Solomon ruled well. He solved problems. He established the kingdom. This man became famous because of his wisdom and his people prospered. When you read of all he accomplished it is utterly amazing.

So, what I don't understand is this: if he was the wisest person in the world, why towards the end of his life didn't wisdom help him make better choices? How could the wisest man in the world make such foolish decisions?

1 Kings 10 describes the splendor of King Solomon's reign, his wealth, majesty, and possessions beyond imagination! But chapter 11:1 begins another account about him using the word "however": "King Solomon, however, loved many foreign women …"

Sometimes I hate the word "however."

Wasn't he wise enough to see the danger in this? God wisely had commanded his people not to marry people from other nations because of the tendency for their hearts to turn away from the one true God to the idols of those nations. And yet, not only did he marry them, "Solomon held fast to them in love" (1 Kgs 11:2).

And so, it happened. His wives led him astray from the one true God.

> As Solomon grew old, his wives turned his heart after other gods, and his heart was not fully devoted to the LORD his God, as the heart of David his father had been. He followed Ashtoreth the goddess of the Sidonians, and Molech the detestable god of the Ammonites. So Solomon did evil in the eyes of the LORD; he did not follow the LORD completely, as David his father had done. (1 Kgs 11:4-6a)

Why didn't wisdom help Solomon see more clearly? What good was all this wisdom if it didn't keep his heart from turning? How big of a part did growing old play in his decision making? How could his idol worshipping wives have such influence over the wisest man in the world? How could someone who started out so well end up so lost? How was it that someone who loved God could leave him to worship detestable idols. Where was the wisdom in that?

And the bigger question for me is this: if the wisest man in the world could end up forsaking God, what hope is there for normal me? I have a bit more wisdom than I used to have, but nothing compared to Solomon.

I have concluded that wisdom can be helpful, but wisdom without obedience is useless.

The advantage King David had over Solomon is highlighted in these same verses. Though David wasn't as wise as his son, David's heart was fully devoted to the Lord, and he followed the Lord completely. He obeyed. His heart was steadfast. And when David sinned, he confessed and still pursued God relentlessly.

If God were to ask me what I wanted, I don't think I would ask for wisdom. I hope I would not ask for riches or honor. It seems it would be better to ask for a heart that would remain fully devoted to him.

I want to finish well. I desire to follow God fully all the days of my life. Maybe wisdom points me to this, but it is obedience that will make it happen.

Scripture

> **And now, Israel, what does the LORD your God ask of you but to fear the LORD your God, to walk in obedience to him, to love him, to serve the LORD your God with all your heart and with all your soul, and to observe the LORD's commands and decrees that I am giving you today for your own good? (Deut 10:12-13)**

Questions

1. What are the benefits of wisdom?

2. Where do you struggle with obedience and how do you live unwisely?

3. What will you put into practice today that will help you finish well?

Prayer

I want to be wise and obedient. May I be aware of my weaknesses and not give into temptations that would lead me away from you. Empower me by your Spirit to live wisely and with a heart that is quick to obey. Help me not to rationalize poor decisions. Help me be more like David than Solomon. Amen.

13

Hands Off My Alabaster Jar!

Jesus didn't ask for Mary's alabaster jar. She wanted to give it to him. She broke her treasure open and poured out her valued perfume to honor her Lord. Mary willingly gave all to Jesus. She didn't hold back or give him just a drop. She poured. She trusted.

Sometimes I give all to God. But often, on the things I want most, I hold back. When I pray, I tell God I want his will, but in my heart I really want mine. The most honest way I can put it is, "God, I *want* to want your will. But I'm scared you'll take what I love away. Help me trust you and love you more."

My first instinct is to try to keep my alabaster jar sealed. Tightly. Away from all-powerful hands that want me to give all when even the thought of giving any is scary. Even when I know it is for my good to do so, I am hesitant. I want at least some control over what I give up.

When I was pregnant with our third child, I went to the doctor because of a possible miscarriage. He said there was nothing I could do but go home and rest. I remember lying on the bed, knowing this was something outside of my control. I could do nothing to ensure that I could keep the baby. I desperately wanted her to be OK. She was in God's hands. But was she safe there?

I remember praying, but my alabaster jar lid was closed. I wanted to keep this treasure. But rather than holding on tightly, I needed to picture my arms open, hands out and palms up, giving my baby to Jesus while asking him to let me keep her. I had no other option but to give this treasure to him and trust. In his mercy and kindness, he blessed us with Kristi about seven months later.

Thirty years later this same daughter lost her longed-for baby. Soon after that my other daughter also had a miscarriage. We prayed for these little ones. I implored the Lord for their lives. He is the same God. Why did he take their treasures? How does he choose when to take and when to give? It is hard to trust him when we think the outcomes determine what we want to give.

There are times when I prayed that I not only kept my alabaster jar sealed tight, but I also tried to hide it. I shielded it with my whole being, trying to protect it from God. Even as I did so, I prayed fervently for what I wanted. It was like praying the opposite of Jesus, "Not thy will, but mine be done." I had no peace. As the Lord worked in my heart, he kept affirming his love for me. Eventually I came to where I could open my arms and pour out my treasure, knowing I could trust God to do what is best.

When Mary poured out perfume from her alabaster jar, she gave it to honor Jesus. Judas and other disciples thought it was wasteful. Yet, Jesus accepted her offering as a beautiful thing. He knew his death was coming. She opened her alabaster jar and poured it out in faith, not fully understanding that it would point to his sacrifice. It wasn't long after this that he was going to pray, as he offered his own alabaster jar to God, "Not my will, but Thine be done."

Jesus saw what the disciples could not. Mary's offering foretold a tragedy. A redeeming tragedy, but still a tragedy. Jesus saw her offering as preparation for his burial. He was going to die. Loss. He would rise from the dead. Gain. God has purpose in how he answers prayers through losses and gains.

How does God choose what to do with our treasures when we pour them out? I don't know. But my soul knows he always does what is best. By faith I continue to learn to trust him when *how* he works doesn't seem best to me. I want to be more like Mary and offer to Jesus all that is in my alabaster box.

No holding back. No keeping it sealed. No hiding the jar.

Open, pour, and trust.

(Note: Jesus was so touched by Mary's expression of love and faith that he wanted her story recorded in memory of her. John 12:1–8; Matt 26:6–13; Mark 14:1–9.)

Scripture

While he was in Bethany, reclining at the table in the home of Simon the Leper, a woman came with an alabaster jar of very expensive perfume, made of pure nard. She broke the jar and poured the perfume on his head.

Some of those present were saying indignantly to one another, "Why this waste of perfume? It could have been sold for more than a year's wages and the money given to the poor." And they rebuked her harshly.

"Leave her alone," said Jesus. "Why are you bothering her? She has done a beautiful thing to me. The poor you will always have with you, and you can help them any time you want. But you will not always have me. She did what she could. She poured perfume on my body beforehand to prepare for my burial. Truly I tell you, wherever the gospel is preached throughout the world, what she has done will also be told, in memory of her." (Mark 14:3–9)

Questions

1. How do you picture your alabaster jar when praying?

2. What makes us hesitate to submit our lives and treasures to the Lord?

3. What have you been protecting from the Lord that you need to entrust to him?

Prayer

It is hard to give to you when I don't trust you. I fear that you will take what I love. When I hear a story of a widow or a parent who loses a child, I am afraid you are preparing me for something similar. I recognize that I can't care for my loved ones like you can. I don't know enough. I'm not powerful enough. I lack control. I trust that your purposes are good. You are good. When I struggle to give you what I love, help me remember what you gave because of your love for me. Amen.

14
A Walk in the Cemetery

We took flowers to my mom's grave last weekend. She was eighty-four when God welcomed her home. As we started walking back to the car, I noticed the gravestone of a high school classmate. He was sixty-three. Walking through a cemetery, we see a variety of years lived. For every grave there is a life story and those left behind who grieve.

There is nothing like walking among the dead to remind us that life is precious. Life is short. No one knows how much time we have in this world. It is a suitable time to think through how we are living and to reflect on what is important. And what is not.

All the things it is easy to long for—money, security, prestige, fame—won't matter. The things that do matter—eternity, relationships, forgiveness—seem easy to ignore! Especially when we focus on those temporary pursuits that cannot satisfy eternal souls.

Graveyards remind us of what is worthwhile. It is a good place to ask ourselves questions. It can be unsettling, but it helps us realign priorities and life ambitions.

Eternity. How is my faith walk with God? Do I long to spend time with him as I did when I first believed in Jesus? I want to keep learning, growing, and loving God more than anything. Now is our only opportunity to walk by faith. One day we will see Jesus and can walk by sight. How is eternity shaping the direction of my life? Death reminds us of what is invaluable in life.

Relationships. The apostle John reminds us of how interwoven our love for God and people is in his first letter. How are my relationships? Can others tell I love God by how I treat people? Is my love for God reflected in my relationship with teammates? Family? Those different from me? Does my love for others demonstrate love for God? Those who have died have no more opportunity on earth to mend or develop new relationships here. The living do. Am I loving in my interactions with friends and strangers?

Forgiveness. Bitterness seems rampant. It is easy to grasp onto grudges and be stingy with forgiveness. As God has forgiven me much, I must remember the grace he's given me and be a conduit of that to others. As long as there is life, there is hope for reconciliation. Once death comes, we can still forgive, but the chance for reconciliation is gone. When believers don't forgive others, we don't model what God has done for us. We weaken our testimony of God's forgiving grace. The light we are called to shine dims when resentment infests our souls.

Cemeteries remind us that death happens to us all. The question we must ask ourselves is, how do we want to live? What will our story be? What is the legacy we want to leave behind?

Scripture

> We love because he first loved us. Whoever claims to love God yet hates a brother or sister is a liar. For whoever does not love their brother and sister, whom they have seen, cannot love God, whom they have not seen. And he has given us this command: Anyone who loves God must also love their brother and sister. (1 John 4:19–21)

Questions

1. What are things that we value here but won't last forever?

2. How have you been a conduit of God's love and grace to others?

3. How have you seen forgiveness worked out where bitterness ruled?

Prayer

Thank you for forgiveness. You have rescued me from eternal damnation. When I'm mad at someone, it is easy to focus on my own hurt and the punishment they deserve for failing me. I'm sorry for forgetting your great mercy. May I love others well and love you more than all. In my short life, may you be well pleased. Amen.

15
Living Eulogies

Eulogies. I have always connected a eulogy with death. When someone dies, people say or write good things about them.

But who says eulogies must wait until someone dies? When my mom went to heaven, I started getting daily grief-share emails[1] that came for one year. I found many of them to be helpful as I dealt with the sadness of missing my mom.

Day 343 talked about living eulogies. In it, Rev. John Coulombe wrote:

> Living eulogies should start at the crib with hands laid on the infants, speaking to them good things about who they are, God's will for them, and God's blessing upon them. Living eulogies should continue through those childhood years and adolescent years and adult years and death years. It should be a lifestyle. A living eulogy is the greatest gift that you can give. It is telling someone he or she has value and wishing God's best upon his or her life.[2]

I had set aside the morning of the one-year anniversary of my mom's death to remember and grieve. I spent time thinking about mom, looking at pictures, listening to music, and thanking God for her life. I don't think I left anything unsaid to my mom. She knew I loved her and appreciated her. Of course, if I had a few more minutes with her, I could tell her more!

For days after that morning, I couldn't forget the concept of living eulogies. I felt inspired to pass on living eulogies to those who are still with me. Why wait until they are gone? It's a bit late to start at the crib with

---

[1] https://www.griefshare.org/.
[2] https://www.griefshare.org/dailyemails/recipients/DYcDW6laS12EHJuPwZXT/messages/343.

my kids since they are all in their thirties or forties! But I could share with them now what I appreciate about them and what I see in them that makes my heart sing. I wrote a living eulogy to each of my kids, their spouses, and my grandkids. My desire is to keep giving them. May I affirm how God has made each person and encourage them in their pursuit of God and his will for them. I am so grateful for how the Lord has made each one. Rather than quietly giving thanks as I pray or think about them, I want to encourage them with what I communicate to them! I wish I had been more intentional with living eulogies for my kids from the cradle through the teens and into adulthood.

We all get plenty of negative messages in the world that point out what we are lacking. We aren't beautiful enough, smart enough, thin enough, powerful enough, wealthy enough. May my family and I know that God has given us all we need to fulfill his purposes for us.

When I see something that I can affirm in friends and co-workers, I can tell them rather than silently applaud them in my head. When I read something that changes me, I can let the person who wrote it know.

The benefits of living eulogies on team life would be incalculable. Relationships are often stretched to the point of breaking. They would grow stronger as we appreciate and affirm one another. Showing value to one another develops a unifying bond that enables us to withstand hardships.

We can be miserly with praise for others. Maybe we are afraid people will become conceited. We could be waiting for praise *from* them before we give out praise *to* them.

My mom can't hear what I say about her now. She isn't here. Eulogies can't encourage her; she doesn't need them as she walks in perfect communion with Jesus. But they can help me as I grieve—putting into words what I appreciated about her can soothe my heart.

Living eulogies, though, can influence people's lives now. We can be looking for ways to encourage those we love with what we write and what we say.

Today is a good day to give a living eulogy!

Scripture

Do not withhold good from those to whom it is due,
> **when it is in your power to act.**
Do not say to your neighbor,
> **"Come back tomorrow and I'll give it to you"—**
> **when you already have it with you.** (Prov 3:27–28)

Questions

1. How could being given a living eulogy encourage you?

2. Why might people be stingy with words of affirmation?

3. Who are the three people you plan to send a living eulogy to?

Prayer

Thank you for the people you put in my life who have helped me grow. Thank you for my family and the blessing of parents who love me. I am grateful for the opportunity to stay connected with my children. Thank you for mentors, teammates, and friends—all those who have influenced me and built into me. Some know how much they have meant to me. Others don't. Help me be quick with words to encourage and affirm. May I be intentional in letting others know how God has used them in my life or the lives of others. Amen.

16
When It Is OK to Talk to Yourself

Quiet. After many years with four kids, and lots of activity and noise, it felt strange when they moved out and silence moved in.

Soon before becoming empty nesters, Don and I were having dinner. It was only the two of us. The kids weren't there to talk or ask for seconds. The quietness felt strange, and I asked him, "Do you think this is how it will be when the kids have all moved out?"

He shrugged.

"Let's make some ground rules," I said. "We have to make verbal responses to questions!" I needed to hear words!

I remember cooking dinner, and no one was running in to grab a snack or ask a question. It was just me and the dinner. For conversation's sake, I opened the oven door and said, "Are you almost done?" I thought that was weird but decided it would only be crazy if the dinner answered back.

The quiet is normal now, and I don't talk aloud to dinners or desserts. I admit, though that I sometimes talk to myself. Not always aloud, but sometimes. As I read Scripture, I see there are others who spoke to themselves. In Psalm 42, the psalmist asked questions to his soul, and in Judges 5, Deborah commanded hers!

The dire situation presented in Psalm 42 describes a person crying night and day. While in distress, people are asking him all day long, "Where is your God?" Not only was his soul weary, but his enemies were incessantly taunting him. Pressures from within and without were assaulting his soul.

With tears streaming, he asks his soul a question and also gives it hope. "Why, my soul, are you downcast? Why so disturbed within me? Put your hope in God, for I will yet praise him, my Savior and my God" (Ps 42:5).

He is speaking truth to his soul to counteract his own sorrow and the verbal uncertainties about God he was hearing. He was saying, "Soul, why are you so sad? You know you can put your hope in God. Have confidence that you *will* yet praise him."

Deborah and Barak are singing a song recounting the battle they had recently won. Reading the account of the battle, you can almost feel the ferocity. They were fighting against nature as the Kishon river was sweeping them away. They were also attacking a mighty army on horseback. Deborah vividly describes it in Judges 5:22, "Then thundered the horses' hooves—galloping, galloping go his mighty steeds." And what does Deborah say in the middle of this song and who does she talk to? She speaks to her soul and says, "March on, my soul; be strong!" (Judg 5:21).

When my problems seem too big for God to handle, my soul is being influenced by lies. It starts to shrink back in fear. My soul begins to feel downcast when hearing news of natural disasters. "March on, my soul; be strong!" There are wars and rumors of wars. "March on, my soul; be strong!" People ask if there is a God, or where he is when evil abounds and hope seems lost. I am swayed and begin to doubt God's goodness and presence. "March on, my soul; be strong!"

Talking to ourselves is sometimes necessary. This is what I am saying to my soul today: "Soul, God is always present, always bigger, always stronger. Don't worry. Trust him."

"March on, my soul; be strong!"

Scripture

> I remember my affliction and my wandering,
>> the bitterness and the gall.
>
> I well remember them,
>> and my soul is downcast within me.
>
> Yet this I call to mind
>> and therefore I have hope:
>
> Because of the LORD's great love we are not consumed,
>> for his compassions never fail.
>
> They are new every morning;
>> great is your faithfulness.
>
> I say to myself, "The LORD is my portion;
>> therefore I will wait for him." (Lam 3:19–24)

Questions

1. If you could tell your soul one truth, what would it long to hear?

2. How can lies influence your attitude towards God and yourself?

3. How can you strengthen your soul?

Prayer

Help me to recognize lies quickly. I know in my head that things like, "You aren't near. You don't care. Life is too hard," are lies. But sometimes my heart feels discouraged because these lies sneak in. Help me not just listen for truth from others, but to speak truth to myself. May I let your word dwell in me richly and as a result my soul be strengthened. Amen.

17
Mopping, Missioning, and Mothering

I was interacting with a woman serving across cultures who had young children. She said she didn't have much time for ministry because she was busy with her children.

I remember thinking along similar lines when I was a young mother and trying to figure out how to balance ministry with family. However, I came to realize that ministry and family are not separate designations; they are both ministry—just ministry in different spheres. It is ministry in the home and ministry outside of it. We need discernment when deciding how much time we invest into which sphere of ministry.

When our children were younger my larger sphere of ministry was in my home. I had a view of what to do outside as well, but time was limited. When they were in preschool, I had mornings for outreach; we sometimes met with others as a family in the evenings. Other times my husband and I would take turns babysitting so one of us could meet with friends. Occasionally we would have a friend come stay with our kids so we could minister as a couple or go out on a date.

Mostly, though, I was home with the kids when they were home. I helped them with homework, took them to the park, watched movies with them, played with them, mothered them, had devotions with them, prayed with them, loved them, and disciplined them. Of course, I did all this imperfectly, with love, a lot of prayer … and some whining! Sometimes I played hide-n-seek with my little ones—partly because it was fun, but also because I needed time to myself. I remember praying while hiding behind the file cabinet before they found me, "Lord, I just need a few minutes alone!"

My husband, too, dedicated time to his ministry in the home and fathering our children. I remember a marked difference in our family as he began to choose more intentionally to minister in our home and not just focus on the ministry outside of it. Balancing time in our spheres of ministry is not just a women's issue—men and women both have a vital ministry in the home. Choosing how much time to invest in each sphere of ministry is something about which mothers and fathers must be purposeful and prayerful. We talked about it together and made some adjustments, but we were never sure we were balancing well. It isn't easy to discern how to juggle all we need and want to do. We look back on the time we invested ministering in our home as an eternally valuable investment of time and energy. Our four children are now parenting their own children and seeking to do so while loving Jesus! We praise God for his amazing kindness, and we thank our children for their forgiveness when we made mistakes.

When the kids were older, I had more time to serve outside my home. I met with friends to talk about spiritual things; we had recipe exchanges where we also shared a devotional. Exercising at an aerobics class and having language exchanges all provided opportunities for sharing the gospel. Though I devoted more of my ministry focus to my home than outside it, the home wasn't my total focus. Serving Jesus was my focus, and that took place both in and out of my home.

There is a third sphere of ministry that takes place in the home that can seem menial and not ministry at all. That is the mopping, the cleaning, the dishes, and the laundry—all those things that threaten to overtake us if we get behind and that are so necessary in caring for ourselves and our family.

We sometimes see these mundane tasks as obstacles to ministry. It can come as a surprise when living overseas how much more time these chores take up than they did in the States. There are often no dryers, so ironing becomes an added chore. Soaking and washing fruits and vegetables, sifting dead bugs from frozen flour, picking through rice for stones, shopping at four markets instead of one supermarket, cooking from scratch out of necessity and not by choice! It all takes time and it's hard to remember that this, too, is ministry. It is caring for family, serving those we love, and ultimately honoring the Lord not only by what we do but how we do it.

Mark wrote about some of the women who followed Jesus: "In Galilee these women had followed him and cared for his needs" (Mark 15:41). I think they did some laundry, cooking, and probably some cleaning. It did not go unnoticed because they did it for Jesus. They served him in practical ways.

Whether we are mopping, missioning, or mothering—or doing all three at the same time—we are serving to honor the Lord.

Scripture

And whatever you do, whether in word or deed, do it all in the name of the Lord Jesus, giving thanks to God the Father through him.

Whatever you do, work at it with all your heart, as working for the Lord, not for men, since you know that you will receive an inheritance from the Lord as a reward. It is the Lord Christ you are serving. (Col 3:17, 23–24)

Questions

1. What are your different spheres of ministry?

2. How do you wisely determine where to invest your time and talents?

3. How does knowing you are serving Christ make a difference in your attitude?

Prayer

Thank you for the privilege of serving you. May I honor you in the mundane tasks as I do them for you. May I honor you whether I work behind the scenes or in the forefront. I desire to wholeheartedly serve and live for you in the little and big, the near and the far, the important and seemingly insignificant opportunities that come my way. Amen.

18
What Is Your Name?

It seems like an easy question, doesn't it? But sometimes, living in this present world, we can confuse who we are—our true identity—with different names that are more dependent on our circumstances or feelings.

I was at a retreat and the worship leader asked us to think about what names we might be giving ourselves. She gave some different options and time to think about it.

She mentioned names like: Lonely, Fearful, Hopeless, Angry, and Overlooked. We were to write down the name we were calling ourselves. I wrote down one of the names that struck home: "Not enough." One of the benefits of growing older is getting to know myself better. Here are two things that I know about me: One of my fears is feeling insignificant. One of my desires is to feel valued.

God knows that about me. He knows me better than I know myself. He knows my weaknesses, my strengths, and how I feel. God sees my fears and desires. Because he knows me so well, he knows what I need. About twenty years ago, he led me to discover some life-changing truths that I needed to know. I learned that my value isn't based on what I do. I could do everything well or fail at everything and it wouldn't change how he values me. I also learned that my worth isn't dependent on what people think of me. If people approve of me wholeheartedly and let me know it, or if they don't like me at all and let me know that—it doesn't change how much God loves me. I'm valued by God simply because he loves me and treasures me as his creation.

However, even as old as I am and as well as I know myself, every now and again questions about my worth sneak up on me based on my desire to be worthwhile.

Have I done enough? Am I useful? How useful am I? When those thoughts invade, the name I call myself is "not enough." My self-talk goes like this, "You aren't useful enough. You should do more. What you have done, you should have done better. You should be more … (fill in the blank)." There are a lot of *shoulds* in my self-talk! They all point to the false thinking that my value is based on what I do.

The next step at the retreat was to share the names we wrote with a friend. We listened to each other as we talked about why we chose those names. Then our assignment was to throw our papers into the fire and pick out a different name for our friend that would counteract lies and state who we are in Christ. Names that are true and say who we really are, not who we fear we are.

My friend gave me the name, "Chosen; fruit bearer (John 15:16)." "You did not choose me, but I chose you, and appointed you so that you might go and bear fruit—fruit that will last—and so that whatever you ask in my name the Father will give you."

God chose me when I was still his enemy. There was nothing in me to lead him to choose me. He just did. God appointed me to go and bear fruit. I can't bear fruit on my own. He knows that. I abide in him and let him work. He has given me a relationship where I can go to the Father and ask for what I need.

I felt free as I released the false name of "not enough." I remembered the truth that "the One who is enough" chose me to be his child.

Maybe like me, at different times you've called yourself by different names.

I can look back and see times when my identity changed. I was fretful when the future was unclear. I was worried when finances were tight. I forgot about God and what he said in his word because I was so focused on my circumstances that my weakness became more of my identity than being God's loved child.

What identities have you been taking on? When you look in the mirror who do you say you are? Worried, discontent, burdened, afraid? Any other names you can think of?

It is beneficial to take some time to consider what names you've been calling yourself. We don't have to be afraid to acknowledge where we are and how we are feeling. God knows. As you looked at the list of names, did you see one that you've been calling yourself? Or maybe there is one not on the list that you've thought of. Whatever name you choose, write it down on a piece of paper.

After you've written it down, take that paper, tear it up, and throw it away in the trash. Then choose a name given in Scripture that is true and forever like Chosen, Comforted, Loved, Citizen of Heaven, Temple of God. If you can't think of a name with a scriptural trait, search out a Bible verse to make your own. Write it down. Keep it with you as a reminder on those days when other names might crowd your thinking and you almost forget who you are in Jesus.

What is your name?

Scripture

> **Whoever has ears, let them hear what the Spirit says to the churches. To the one who is victorious, I will give some of the hidden manna. I will also give that person a white stone with a new name written on it, known only to the one who receives it.** (Rev 2:17)

Questions

1. What are the more common names you call yourself?

2. How have you struggled with feelings of insignificance?

3. What is the truth about who you are in Christ?

Prayer

Thank you for truth. You know me. You love me. You made me. God, you see the depths of my heart where fears and insecurities dwell. May I remember truth when I feel discouraged about my weaknesses and think that my value rests on being strong. Help me recognize lies before I lose hope. My confidence is in you. You have given me power to overcome and a solid foundation on which to stand. You are more than enough when I feel like I am not enough. Amen.

19
One Foot in the Air

A huge army came to fight against Asa, and we read his response:

> Then Asa called to the LORD his God and said, "LORD, there is no one like you to help the powerless against the mighty. Help us, LORD our God, for we rely on you, and in your name we have come against this vast army. LORD, you are our God; do not let mere mortals prevail against you." (2 Chron 14:11)

God gave victory. It thrills my heart to read how Asa relied upon God when he was feeling powerless and how God intervened. Asa worked diligently to follow hard after God. It is written in 2 Chronicles 15:17, "Asa's heart was fully committed to the LORD all his life."

What happened to Asa between chapters 15 and 16? After thirty-six years (36!) of experiencing God's faithfulness, when enemies came this time, he didn't seek God. He sought military help from unbelievers and did not trust the Lord. When confronted by a prophet about this, Asa was so angry he threw the prophet in jail. He went on to brutally oppress the people. When he got desperately sick, he still didn't seek the Lord for healing. He limited himself to human help.

After so many years of faithfulness to God, did Asa become complacent? Was he proud? Had he become overconfident in himself? Did he forget about God? How did he turn from wholeheartedly following God to getting sidetracked towards the end of his life?

I desire to remain dogged in my pursuit of God, ever reliant on his grace. As I've thought about ways to do this, I came up with some obvious strategies:

- Stay in the word of God.
- Keep praying.
- Practice spiritual disciplines.
- Take risks that make me uncomfortable and force me to keep trusting God.
- When hard things come my way, seek God's help first.

One other thing I've been thinking about as I grow older and am experiencing loss more often, is to think about death. Not to fear it nor to anticipate it, but to recognize it as a certainty. Philip Yancey wrote this in *Where Is God When It Hurts*:

> In short, because of our belief in a home beyond, Christians can be realistic about death without becoming hopeless. Death is an enemy, but a defeated enemy. As Martin Luther told his followers, "Even in the best of health we should have death always before our eyes [so that] we will not expect to remain on this earth forever, but will have one foot in the air, so to speak."[1]

I like the picture of living with one foot in the air! This means having one foot here on earth. Choosing to live life to the fullest while seeking to honor God in everything. But I must remember that I also have one foot in the air. Knowing life is short and death will come affects the choices I make today.

Living with one foot in the air helps me consider long-term effects of short-term decisions. It keeps me more focused on the Lord and his calling, not my own desires. My heart is prone to forget about God. When things are going well it is way too easy to depend on my own strength. And think it is effective! May I listen to the voice of God. By his grace, may I choose to rely on his Word. Recognizing my weakness, I must seek his power.

As I do this, he will keep me balanced as my two feet are firmly planted in two different worlds. One foot is in this world and the other is ready for the next.

---

[1] Philip Yancey, *Where Is God When It Hurts* (Grand Rapids: Zondervan, 1978), 256.

Scripture

Show me, LORD, my life's end
    and the number of my days;
    let me know how fleeting my life is.
You have made my days a mere handbreadth;
    the span of my years is as nothing before you.
Everyone is but a breath,
    even those who seem secure.
Surely everyone goes around like a mere phantom;
    in vain they rush about, heaping up wealth
    without knowing whose it will finally be.
But now, Lord, what do I look for?
    My hope is in you. (Ps 39:4–7)

Questions

1. What does living with one foot in the air look like to you?

2. How do you maintain a vigorous walk with God?

3. What needs to change to keep an eternal focus while living in the here and now?

Prayer

Life is short. I can't believe I'm in the second half of life. It has gone by so quickly. Keep me attentive to growing in my walk with you. May I listen to your Spirit and be quick to obey his prompting. Keep me loving your word and may my prayer life keep developing so that my walk with you is vibrant. May I never plateau but always want a deeper connection with you. Amen.

20

Bracing

John wrote, "I have told you these things, so that in me you may have peace. In this world you will have trouble. But take heart! I have overcome the world" (John 16:33).

Some of Jesus's statements are encouraging. Many are comforting. Others warn us. In this verse we have all three. Jesus encourages us that we can have peace in him. I am comforted when he tells me to take heart because he has overcome the world. Jesus is also bracing his followers when he warns us of trouble in this world.

Years ago, in the Middle East, our team leaders were planning a retreat. They visited the coastal town to check it out. The beach was nice, but the sea was teeming with jellyfish. When they came back, they told us what we needed to bring and what it was like. They also told us about the jellyfish. More than once, they reminded us of the jellyfish. When we got there, yes there were jellyfish. After the retreat they asked people to fill out an evaluation form about the retreat. No one complained about the jellyfish. Did we like them? No. Were they bothersome? Yes. Did people get stung? Indeed.

Why did no one complain?

Because we were braced. We knew trouble was coming and it wasn't a surprise.

Jesus does the same for us. In this world you will have trouble. Why have I been so surprised at how hard ministry can be? The work is challenging and tiring—physically, emotionally, and spiritually. Why is that startling? Looking through Paul's epistles, he often mentions his or his co-laborers' labor. He talks about toil, struggles, and hard work in ministry. Why are we surprised when we encounter hardships in working across cultures? It is strenuous!

Many of us coming from the west seem to expect (or at least desire) comfort. When trials come, we realize that comfort is a higher value than we realized. Our calling isn't to ease, but to the faith stretching walk of obedience. We easily forget about Jesus's call to die to self, take up our cross daily, and follow him.

Walking by faith is hard as it goes against the world's system. Serving across cultures is difficult, but part of our calling is to follow where God leads. Jesus doesn't sugar coat the truth. He braces us for challenges. He tells us these things, so that in him we may have peace. Peace during whatever we face. His peace is not found only in the absence of conflict. His peace is not dependent on external circumstances, but on his eternal presence no matter what else is going on.

Someone said that peace is not the absence of storms, but God's presence in the storm. Sometimes the storm comes in opposition to ministry. Other times storms happen when relationships shatter. Our own choices can lead us into storms. And storms can come to us. It doesn't matter if we are married or single, young or old. It doesn't even matter where we serve. Everyone faces challenges. What gives us hope as believers is that in Jesus we have peace in every storm.

In the Bible, God is called our rock, our refuge, our strong tower, our anchor—all things that picture steadiness and protection in the middle of upheaval. Whatever storms we are facing today, Jesus knew they were coming. He warned us of trouble.

Take heart! The Lord promises peace. He has overcome the world.

Scripture

Truly my soul finds rest in God;

    my salvation comes from him.

Truly he is my rock and my salvation;

    he is my fortress, I will never be shaken. (Ps 62:1–2)

Questions

1. What troubles have you been facing?

2. How has God been a rock for you in the midst of storms?

3. How can you play a role in bracing others for challenges in life and ministry?

Prayer

I have felt shaken, but I am so thankful that I can never be shaken loose from you. You have a firm hold on my life. I am secure. Thank you, Jesus, for bracing me to expect troubles while at the same time assuring me of peace in the midst of them. My life isn't about my comfort but about your glory. May I remember this truth when storms come. Remind me of your presence today as I face its troubles. I leave tomorrow's concerns in your hands. Amen.

21
Therapy

Physical therapy and spiritual growth are a lot alike. I discovered this after my fall in the airport when I fractured my left kneecap and right arm bone. When my arm cast had been off for about one month, it still hurt to type, text, or move. I couldn't carry anything in my right hand. I had learned to do many things with my left hand—eat, brush my teeth, brush my hair. Write! My prayer journal looked like a child wrote it.

I became more ambidextrous than before, although I still wasn't good with my left hand. But time passed and my arm strength grew. It felt good to write again using complete sentences as I communicated my heart to God. My leg brace came off after my arm cast. After six weeks of not bending my knee, it hurt to bend it even a little. I started therapy, but getting my knee to work again wasn't easy.

I am more susceptible to discouragement when I am in pain. Progress seems beyond my ability. Unable to do even simple things makes it worse. Tears of frustration flowed when I couldn't take the one little step up to take a longed-for shower. Finally able to go out with friends, I walked too much and came home exhausted and sore. I tried to find the balance between attempting too much and doing too little. One ended in pain and more tears. The other didn't help me improve, which would make recovery a longer process. But I know (theoretically) with hard work and practice, I will get better. I just needed to convince my knee! Others who have injured their knees or gotten knee replacements are leading normal lives. My physical therapist encouraged me to keep at it. Seeing progress, even small doses, kept me going.

At times in my spiritual life, I also grow discouraged. When circumstances are hard, I slip into unhealthy ways of dealing with stress, and prayer loses its appeal because God seems distant. I lose fervor; I grow weary. I think, "I should be stronger than this," and guilt forces its way into the fray. Vibrancy for life, for God, for everything, dims.

But I've been discouraged before, and God has led me through. I see others who have struggled, and they have modeled stick-to-God faith and experienced his faithfulness. I will keep reading his word and keep praying even when it feels useless.

Working through pain or discouragement could be called "spiritual therapy"—walking when hurting, trusting when fearful, persevering when feeling overwhelmed. Sometimes difficulties seem huge, and God seems small. Therapy takes time and hard work. So does walking by faith and trusting God with each step of reliance on him.

Scripture

But as for me, I watch in hope for the LORD,

> **I wait for God my Savior;**
>
> **my God will hear me.**

Do not gloat over me, my enemy!

> **Though I have fallen, I will rise.**

Though I sit in darkness,

> **the LORD will be my light.** (Mic 7:7–8)

Questions

1. What are the challenges of any type of therapy?

2. How has God encouraged you during a trial?

3. How can we walk alongside others through their challenges?

Prayer

Recovery always takes longer than I think it should. I would love instant healing and an automatic close walk with you. Most things that are worthwhile in life take a lot of arduous work. So, it is with a walk of faith. May I seek you daily and remember that I run this race until the finish line. May I not grow weary or lose heart but help me keep my eyes on Jesus. Amen.

22
Selfish Ambition

Public speaking was one of my favorite classes in high school and college. Mentors at church opened doors for me to teach young people and plan Bible studies for youth. I remember standing behind the pulpit in an empty church and thinking how cool it would be to speak to audiences about Jesus. I have loved almost every opportunity I've had to speak as well as all God teaches me in preparing for those times of teaching. I am always a bit nervous but am thrilled when I get to teach God's word.

A few years ago, I was being considered as a speaker for a women's event. The director of this ministry came and heard me speak at another conference. I wanted to do a really good job so that I would be invited to speak at her event. After my "trial run" I waited and waited to hear back from her but didn't. I prayed about it. I tried being patient. Didn't I do well? Was I not a good communicator? I thought I was gifted in this area. But maybe not. I really, really, *really* wanted to speak at this event.

As I was having my quiet time one morning, I remember interacting with God about this and ardently sharing my desire (yet again) to speak at this event. I sensed that he was asking me this question, "Sue, if you are not the best person for this particular audience and if I can use someone else more effectively, do you still want to do this?" I knew that yes was the wrong answer, but I still longed to do it!

However, at around this same time I had been reading in Philippians and came to verses 2:3–4, "Do nothing out of selfish ambition or vain conceit, but in humility consider others better than yourselves. Each of you should look not only to your own interests, but to the interests of others."

How much of my desire was selfish ambition? Was I seeking value based on what I did rather than my identity in Jesus? Did I just like the idea of speaking and being in front of people? Did I like the attention more than I wanted to serve? I told God I certainly did *not* want to be the one speaking if someone else could be more effective and helpful to others. I asked him to use whoever they chose (and he chose) to speak and to abundantly bless her ministry.

Spending time in prayer is an effective way to examine myself and fight against selfish ambition. When I am tempted to feel envious of other people with opportunities that I wish I had, I feel convicted, and I pray. God is at work in me and empowers me to thank God for opportunities to serve him that come my way. I also pray for others who are doing what I love to do and doing it by God's invitation and grace. I pray that God will bless their ministries, open more doors for them, and give them even more opportunities to use their gifts for his glory.

It was some time after I had been praying for this women's event and God's blessing on it that the invitation came to speak there. Thankfully, by then my desire was to do God's will and honor him, and any hint of selfish ambition had been defeated.

How we serve God is much less important than actually knowing him. Do you remember the time when the disciples went out and were healing the sick and casting out demons? They were all excited about what they could do, but Jesus replied to them that true joy comes in *knowing* him.

We can be thankful that God gives us gifts, but let's praise him *even more* for the forgiveness of our sins and the miracle that our names are written in heaven. We actually know God, the creator of the entire universe; we became his children when we trusted in Jesus as our Savior.

He has gifted each one of us to serve him. Whether we teach, lead, show mercy or give, it is only by God's grace and power and it is always for his glory. How thrilling to serve God and use the gifts he has chosen to give us.

Ultimately though, our most joyous honor is to be his children!

Scripture

> The seventy-two returned with joy and said, "Lord, even the demons submit to us in your name."
>
> He replied, "I saw Satan fall like lightning from heaven. I have given you authority to trample on snakes and scorpions and to overcome all the power of the enemy; nothing will harm you. However, do not rejoice that the spirits submit to you, but rejoice that your names are written in heaven." (Luke 10:17–20)

Questions

1. How does selfish ambition exhibit itself in your life?

2. How can we combat selfish ambition?

3. How long has it been since you thanked God for his gift of salvation to you?

Prayer

I hate the thought that selfish ambition steals its way into my heart and distorts my motivation to serve you. Help me to recognize it quickly and always pray for those whose ministry you are blessing in places I'd long to serve. May I seek to do your will above all else. I thank you that my name is written in heaven and that my home is with you. Knowing you is my true source of joy, don't let me be deceived into thinking that serving you is more important than knowing you. Amen.

23
Running, Deception, and Spiritual Grit

When I met Don in college, I loved being with him. He invited me to go running with him. I hated to run, but I loved him. And so, I ran. Fast forward to our honeymoon. We were at a state park in Kentucky. We had rented a cute little cabin near a small lake. It was a lovely sunny day and my new husband asked, "Want to go running?" "Sure," I replied. I put on my shorts and tee shirt, tied my tennis shoes, and stepped outside. It was hot and I really did hate to run. I didn't have to run to be with him—we would have a lifetime together. I remember starting out with him and seeing a bench. "I don't want to run. I will wait here for you," I said to my surprised husband. I haven't run with him, except through airports, in over forty-five years.

When our kids heard that story, they looked at their dad and asked, "Didn't you feel deceived?" Whoa. I never meant to deceive anyone. It was more like a compliment, right? I wanted to be with him so much that I ran! Running is hard work.

Hating to run might have begun in sixth grade. I was in a race and I was going to lose. I was falling further behind as others in my gym class sprinted ahead. I tried … for a while. But when I saw that I wasn't going to be first (or anywhere close to it), I gave up. I walked and acted like I didn't care. But I did. Physically, I could have kept running, but I lacked the spunk to keep trying. When I compared myself to others and wasn't winning, pride won. Fortitude lost. I was gritless.

Whenever I hear the word grit, it is easy to picture running because it is one of the hardest things ever and I would need grit to do it. Fortitude, resolution, pluck, and courage are some synonyms for grit.

I'm not always without grit. Cross-cultural living is not simple. When ministry across cultures is hard, my gut reaction is always a desire to quit. Language learning. Cultural mishaps. Witnessing failures. Team discord. Opposition. Lack of desired progress. Comparing myself to others and feeling inadequate. Being inadequate. But I have been persevering in ministry for more than thirty-seven years. How can that be? I discovered that my own strength is never enough to inspire spiritual grit.

I daily need the grace and power of God. He uses his word to produce spiritual grit in me. It is Scripture that anchors my soul. Talking with the Lord and listening to him is vital. Writing out my prayers in a journal has been life-giving and helps me focus on my interaction with God. Encouraging words from others have held me steady. Confessing my sins and claiming forgiveness is a needed practice. Sharing my weaknesses and burdens so that others know how to pray for me is imperative. Knowing I am feeble and being aware of my weaknesses makes me rely more on the Lord than on myself. I ask the Holy Spirit to fill me and use me as I surrender my will to God's. Grit can be developed!

Scripture uses the image of running a race to portray spiritual grit. I can't seem to get away from running! But this is a different kind of running. Whether we like to run or not, we are in a race. We focus on Jesus as we run. He is the only One able to help us persevere in this race. It isn't a race against others. It is a race we run together toward Jesus. We keep going to finish well.

Spiritual grit is *from* God and *for* God. Because of him, I will run the race. With joy. Jesus is waiting at the finish line. This is a race worth running!

Scripture

> Therefore, since we are surrounded by such a great cloud of witnesses, let us throw off everything that hinders and the sin that so easily entangles. And let us run with perseverance the race marked out for us, fixing our eyes on Jesus, the pioneer and perfecter of faith. For the joy set before him he endured the cross, scorning its shame, and sat down at the right hand of the throne of God.
>
> (Heb 12:1–2)

Questions

1. How is grit evidenced in your life?

2. What are ways to keep your eyes on Jesus while running your race?

3. What are some hindrances and sins that you must throw off in order to run well?

Prayer

May I keep my eyes on you. It is so easy to look around at others. Some are running faster; others run slower. I look around at my situation and circumstances rather than keeping my eyes on you as I run. Remind me that I am in a race that requires perseverance. You ran your race because you knew the joy that was coming. May I run my race well. Amen.

24
Changing Roles and Tangled Emotions

After fifteen years in the same role, I am transitioning from it. I know the timing is good, but I also know transitions are never easy. My emotions fluctuate. I am grieving losses and miss what I did. I am adjusting to new normals and relishing new opportunities. I feel sad and happy at the same time!

There is grief in letting go of what I know and have enjoyed doing for a long time. I was comfortable. I've loved big picture thinking and the opportunities to meet so many of our co-workers around the world. I enjoyed knowing what to do and having my routine. I've relished regular interaction with other women leaders and building those relationships. I will miss the comfort of the known. Transition is moving from what is mostly known to what is less known. My soul twinges in uneasiness. I will miss what was.

Promise and life fills the future; however, the path to get there appears foggy. Walking into the unknown feels unsettling.

The unknown doesn't always feel scary. I also get excited. There is hopeful dreaming of what is to come. I have a few projects in mind that excite me. Writing and developing more resources. Mentoring others. Teaching and training opportunities. The prospect of investing in those newer to cross-cultural service energizes me. It is thrilling to think that I can use what I have learned through life and ministry to walk alongside others in their ministry journeys around the world. The ripple effect is appealing. My heart beats a little faster. I anticipate what could be.

Forging ahead through grief and with hope, it is sometimes confusing to separate who I am from what I do. I am learning that my value to God isn't based on what I do. God doesn't love me more when I do well and love me less when I fail. He loved me when I was his enemy. He loves me as his daughter. His love never fluctuates. It is constant. The ministry roles I have do not define me. My position or title doesn't indicate my worth. What matters is who I serve and my relationship with him.

As I transition into another chapter of ministry, I plan to focus on three short reminders. I jotted them down in my prayer journal, so I won't forget. They are true through every stage of life and ministry, but vital to contemplate as I move onward. These reminders are: in your ways, by your power, and for your glory.

In your ways: God's ways are different from mine. He has a much larger perspective. His perfect plan uses people and world events to accomplish his purposes. I confess, I do not always understand his plan. But depending on my own wisdom and wanting my own way is foolhardy. I choose God's ways (Isa 55:8–9).

By your power: I cannot do things on my own. Jesus said, "I am the vine; you are the branches. If you remain in me and I in you, you will bear much fruit; apart from me you can do nothing" (John 15:5). I am *not* the vine; I am a branch. Even on my good days I am not enough. My strength is puny; my will power is not dependable. The Lord must empower life and ministry. I recognize my limitations, and by his grace, I remain in him.

For your glory: This life isn't about me. My gifts. My roles. My contributions. My vision. My past, present or future. I can have all these things, but none of them are for me or because of me. I am not in competition with others to see who is "the greatest in the kingdom of heaven." All I have is from God. As I recognize that and choose to trust him through everything, he will be honored. I desire his glory.

Transition is another opportunity to walk by faith as a follower of Jesus—whether it feels right or all wrong, when we miss the comfortable and are leery about the unknowns, when we are scared or excited—whatever we are feeling, by faith we take the next step trusting in the One who goes before us.

In his ways, by his power, and for his glory.

Scripture

Oh, the depth of the riches of the wisdom and knowledge of God!
> How unsearchable his judgments,
> and his paths beyond tracing out!

"Who has known the mind of the Lord?
> Or who has been his counselor?"

"Who has ever given to God,
> that God should repay them?"

For from him and through him and for him are all things.
> To him be the glory forever! Amen. (Rom 11:33–36)

Questions

1. What are the biggest stressors for you in transition?

2. How do you grieve losses well?

3. What does it look like to abide in Christ?

Prayer

Transitions are hard, even though I know that what I am going through is normal. I miss what was. I'm not sure what is ahead. Help me not to cling to what has been but look forward to what will be, knowing you lead and empower me. I want to abide in you and look to you so that you are honored in everything about me. Thank you for being my anchor in the sea of change. Amen.

25
Informal Mentoring

We arrived overseas for our first term. I unknowingly assumed that getting there was the biggest adventure. I thought after joining our agency, receiving training, raising support, and getting our visas, passports, shots all in one year that the rest would come more naturally.

I was wrong. There was so much more.

At a grocery store, I bought little packages of dried onions and thought that would be convenient for some of my recipes. In the kitchen as I got the bag out, I realized the onions were moving. As I looked closer, the onions weren't moving, but little insects living among them were. Appalled and disgusted, I called MaryAnn and asked her what to do. She told me to put the bag in the freezer, the cold would kill the bugs and then just use it and forget about the bugs. I thanked her, ended the call, and threw the bag away.

I think she was letting me know that life was going to be different. I would need to adjust. But at that point I just couldn't eat the bugs, even if they were dead. (I never told MaryAnn I threw them away, but she probably knew.)

Our team celebrated birthdays monthly. MaryAnn's birthday was in December and a new teammate arrived who also had a December birthday. As we gathered around the cake she jokingly groaned, "I've always had to share my birthday with Jesus and now I have to share it with you too!" Her sense of humor was delightfully down to earth. I learned from her that humor is good and necessary when serving across cultures and experiencing stress.

We were traveling in one of the many taxis of our host city. MaryAnn was in the front seat, three of us were in the back. This taxi was old—they were all old—but this one was almost ancient! The front passenger door would fly open whenever we turned a corner. Without batting an eye, she simply reached out her arm and shut it again.

I watched and learned to expect the unexpected and deal with it.

After going to the hospital and meeting with a doctor about my baby daughter's head injury, I kept it all together. Dealing with the medical visit alone was emotionally draining and I felt spent. I found out my daughter had a hematoma, not the brain tumor I had feared. She needed no treatment. I headed to MaryAnn's house and knocked on her door. She opened the door, and I couldn't hold back my tears any longer. She held out her arms to take Katie and comfort me.

I learned that it was OK to cry in front of teammates and that teammates take care of each other.

When we returned to the US to work in our agency's office, MaryAnn was the Director of Women's Ministry, and I was her assistant. We worked together on projects, and she invited me into what she was doing. She was not territorial; she was kingdom-minded. She gave me opportunities to develop my gifts. She listened to me when my heart felt like it was breaking and, by God's grace, she kept me focused on Christ.

I blossomed under a leader who sought to help her follower flourish.

MaryAnn did all of this during her own battles. She, too, had mothered children overseas and transitioned back to her home country. She passionately challenged mission agencies to fully utilize and care for their women members. She had serious health concerns, and I watched her battle those with grace. With wonder I saw that she never became self-absorbed. She cared for others. She has now passed from this temporary life to her eternal home. MaryAnn is with her Savior who redeemed her soul and used her life to influence future generations from all walks of life for his glory.

I watched her live and I mourn her passing. She enriched my life and mentored me well—whether she meant to or not. She was available. She listened. She lived out what she believed. She loved well. She gave what she had.

As one who was being mentored, I gained a great deal from watching and listening to her. I know there are more formal and intentional mentorships, and we need to pursue those as well. But often we can benefit from a more informal, life-on-life mentoring. We just need to be open to the opportunities that come our way to give and receive, to learn and to grow, to bless and be blessed.

Scripture

For we know, brothers and sisters loved by God, that he has chosen you, because our gospel came to you not simply with words but also with power, with the Holy Spirit and deep conviction. You know how we lived among you for your sake. You became imitators of us and of the Lord, for you welcomed the message in the midst of severe suffering with the joy given by the Holy Spirit. And so you became a model to all the believers in Macedonia and Achaia. The Lord's message rang out from you not only in Macedonia and Achaia—your faith in God has become known everywhere. (1 Thess 1:4–8a)

Questions

1. How have you benefitted from a mentor?

2. What opportunities are there for you to mentor someone?

3. How can we show our gratitude to those who have mentored us?

Prayer

Thank you for MaryAnn. Thank you for mentors throughout my life. Barb, Frank, Uncle Bob, Phyllis. I can look back and see how you have used people to benefit my walk with you. Mentors who walked along side me, encouraging and exhorting me. Thank you for the privilege you've given me to mentor others, to pass on what you've taught me. Thank you for a rich history of experiencing your faithfulness and goodness. I am grateful to be in your family with people who love and serve you. Amen.

26
Though His Footprints Are Unseen

God always holds my hand but sometimes leaves no footprints.

The psalmist was in distress. He couldn't sleep. He was crying out to God. His present was awful, and tomorrow's unknowns didn't look all that inviting. But he remembered God and began recounting the history of God's provision. He reminded himself of how mighty God is. He recalled how the Lord worked miracles and displayed his holiness through his ways.

He recollected that it was the Lord who led his people to escape from Egypt in days gone by. God would also be his hope for today.

He wrote in Psalm 77:19, "Your path led through the sea, your way through the mighty waters, though your footprints were not seen."

As God led his people through the Red Sea, they saw water piled up on either side of them. As they walked, they did not see evidence of God going in front of them. They saw no footprints. But they were forging ahead through a parted sea into the unknown.

When the dawn of a new year approaches, we don't know what lies ahead. People were in a hurry to say goodbye to 2020—I admit it wasn't my favorite year due to the pandemic—but 2019 was rough for me, too. That was the year my mom died, and I fell and broke two bones. We wonder if next year will be better. Perhaps not. We don't know.

What we do know, is that God goes ahead of us, and though we may not see his footprints, we can keep going because he is leading. There may be sweet surprises, wonderful opportunities, significant conversations. There may also be unexpected turns, screeching halts, and overwhelming challenges. I will forge ahead by faith in the one who goes before me and is always with me. The one who always holds my hand but sometimes leaves no footprints.

I remember all that God has done for his people. Events throughout the Bible remind me of God's grace and power. My own past reveals to me God's faithfulness as time after time he was my refuge and help. I didn't always see evidence of his hand or feel his presence. But he was there. Ever-present.

As we enter new years, we can celebrate with confidence. We can never go where God hasn't been. There isn't a time in history when God was not in charge. We may find ourselves embracing joyous times or enduring bleak circumstances. One thing we can be sure of: God is with us leading the way. His footprints are right in front of us. We simply can't seem them.

We follow by faith.

Scripture

"Will the Lord reject forever?

    Will he never show his favor again?

Has his unfailing love vanished forever?

    Has his promise failed for all time?

Has God forgotten to be merciful?

    Has he in anger withheld his compassion?"

Then I thought, "To this I will appeal:

    the years when the Most High stretched out his right hand.

I will remember the deeds of the LORD;

    yes, I will remember your miracles of long ago.

I will consider all your works

    and meditate on all your mighty deeds. (Ps 77:7–12)

Questions

1. How do you handle doubts and fears about what God is doing?

2. How would you describe a walk of faith?

3. What is an example of God's faithfulness to you that encourages you to keep trusting him today?

Prayer

I know you are good. I am certain you are faithful. When troubles come, my heart often questions what you are doing. I jump to doubting your character. I don't understand some of the heartaches. I can't see your footprints and it seems like life would be easier if I could. But I choose to trust you today. I am grateful for your faithfulness in the past and how you were at work in me and for me throughout my life. Thank you for the privilege of walking by faith. Amen.

27
The Walking Stick

Our guide greeted us, "Welcome to the forest preserve! I look forward to being your guide on the hike. We have some walking sticks here for your use if you would like one."

I enjoy walking. I have a regular walking routine and felt like I was in pretty good shape. I wouldn't need the walking stick. So, I thanked him politely, but declined.

Before starting our walk through the woods, the guide gave us a tour inside their museum. It depicted the history of the forest. Displays showed how their country is preserving and protecting their environment. It was interesting and informative, but I was ready for exploring outside. As he finished the inside tour, our guide said, "Many people use walking sticks on the hike. We have some that are available."

I responded, "That's quite alright. Thank you, though." Before leaving I went to the restroom. It was going to take about an hour and a half to complete the trek through the forest. As we all gathered outside the museum to get started the guide said, "Hiking sticks can be very useful. Here are some in case you are interested."

Finally, I heard what he was saying. If he mentioned something three times, he must have had a very good reason and keen insight into what was to come. He was being very polite in the way he offered the walking sticks. He saw my gray hair and knew some of the challenges ahead. He was trying to ensure I would be OK and have what I needed to stay safe. I had never visited this forest; I had never hiked these trails. I didn't know what the terrain would be like. I was ignorant. The guide was an expert. He knew what was coming and that the stick would come in handy.

The third time I said, "Yes, please. I will use a walking stick." I still didn't believe that I would need it. But he was persistent, and I complied. Reluctantly.

It wasn't too far into the hike that I thanked God I listened to the guide. Climbing over rocks, roots, broken tree limbs would have been tricky without that stick. Uneven terrain was challenging. I would have fallen into the trickling brook without my walking stick. It helped me balance as I forged ahead. What was I thinking? I assumed I had all the skill and help I needed and was ready to dismiss the advice of someone who knew more than me!

When I don't listen to others, when I assume I know best, I often make things harder than they need to be. Thinking we know more than we do can be dangerous. Not listening to others is foolish. Even if we think we know best, it is beneficial to listen to others. Gaining their perspectives helps us choose how to proceed with more wisdom.

It is easy to dismiss what others say if we are overconfident or proud. Solomon warns us about the dangers of pride. Here are two examples of what he wrote:

> Pride goes before destruction, a haughty spirit before a fall. (Prov 16:18)

> Pride brings a person low, but the lowly in spirit gain honor. (Prov 29:23)

Had I not listened to our guide and hiked without my walking stick, pride would have had these exact effects. I would have fallen and been brought low!

Scripture

The way of fools seems right to them,

but the wise listen to advice. (Prov 12:15)

Questions

1. How is pride evident in your life?

2. What are resources available to us for sound advice?

3. How do you discern whether to modify your plan when others advise a different strategy?

Prayer

Keep my heart from pride. May I humbly listen well to others and diligently pursue your will. Sometimes opinions will vary. It is hard to know what to do. May I listen well to others, but wholeheartedly heed your voice. I want to learn and grow, to be wise. Protect me from thinking I know it all. Amen.

28
Life-Long Faith, Grit, and Grace

We are relocating, not to be confused with retiring, retreating, or resigning. We are moving from ministry overseas to serving in my home country. This transition has caused questions to bombard my soul. Will we continue to have enough support? Will God provide? How will we adapt? Why is this so hard? What other challenges will we face? And can we handle them?

All at once, it hit me. These were similar questions to those I asked in 1986 when we left to go overseas for our first term! We weren't sure if people would continue to support us. How would we handle learning a new language and adapting to a new culture? What would it be like? We faced challenges that I didn't expect as well as those we heard about in our pre-field training. But even those we were prepared for were harder than I expected.

Our plan was to serve in one country until God called us home. When God shut that door and opened another, we were sad to leave. We finally had seen a small church begin. And I wondered, "Will I ever be happy again?" After two years in the next country, we were led to leave and work at the Christar US office. Again, I wondered about being happy. Our whole family felt the trauma of that move. After twelve years, we sensed God leading us overseas again. I felt heartbroken as I said goodbye to our children and grandchildren. As the tears flowed, I asked, "Will I ever be happy again?" Sadness invaded each transition, yet in every move, I also felt the joyful anticipation of being where God wanted us to be.

As I look back, we've lived and served on four different continents. *God provided for us.* We've gained ministry and life experience. *God was with us.* I am older and hopefully a bit wiser. *God gives grace.* Now, my circumstances have changed again. In transitions, questions emerge that serve to teach me yet again that our walk of faith lasts a lifetime. *God is trustworthy.*

The same God who provided for me in the beginning will provide for me now *and* in the future. Though countries, homes and circumstances may change, God doesn't. We walked by faith when we were younger and continue to walk by faith as we age. This life on earth is our only chance to walk by faith. We will see Jesus one day and walk by sight, but until then, we trust him step by step, move by move, age to age.

May God encourage us to grow in faith as we trust him throughout our life-long journey of faith.

Scripture

Therefore, since we have a great high priest who has ascended into heaven, Jesus the Son of God, let us hold firmly to the faith we profess. For we do not have a high priest who is unable to empathize with our weaknesses, but we have one who has been tempted in every way, just as we are—yet he did not sin. Let us then approach God's throne of grace with confidence, so that we may receive mercy and find grace to help us in our time of need.

(Heb 4:14–16)

Questions

1. What questions do you ask now that are similar to the ones you asked earlier?

2. How does knowing that God doesn't change help you through life changes?

3. How have you seen your faith grow this past year?

Prayer

I can hold firmly to my faith and approach your throne in confidence knowing you will welcome me. Jesus, I'm so thankful you can empathize with my humanness. You know what it is to be tempted. You know everything about me. I know that you are totally trustworthy. You have always taken care of me, and I can entrust all my needs to you. I am grateful. Amen.

29
Transition, Grumbling, and Gratitude

Transitions are not easy, even with previous experience. Moving from one place and adapting to another, even when it is familiar, is challenging. I've moved back to my passport country—the place where I longed to be on those hard days while living overseas. And yet, here I sometimes find myself longing to go back to the place I called home for almost eight years.

I don't complain all the time. I am happy to be here. I'm excited to be closer to family and anticipate the continuing ministries God has for us. I am fluent in the language here. The culture is familiar. I can hop in a car and drive wherever I want to go. I go to church and enjoy time with old friends.

However, transition does bring out the grumbler in me. I complain more easily because I feel off-kilter due to so many changes. Even though I trust God has led us this direction at this time, I catch myself whining. The weather is colder. The sun doesn't shine 330 days out of the year like it did where we were living. Things are more expensive here. Sticker shock greets me in almost every aisle at the grocery store. Changing insurance companies has been difficult to navigate with many rules and forms. Moving interrupts my used-to-be normal daily routines. I miss my friends, our apartment, our ministries, my favorite outdoor cafe with a perfect cup of coffee topped off with foamy milk.

Today I realized how much I've been grumbling. More than that, I also felt convicted about my lack of gratitude. This imbalance has provided fertile soil from which a complaining spirit has blossomed.

I don't like complaining. I have often harshly judged the Israelites who complained in the wilderness after they escaped slavery in Egypt.

They were following Moses to the promised land. But, on the way through the challenging times, they wanted to go back to Egypt. They remembered only the good things in their former home. It seemed better to return there as slaves than to roam free in the wilderness. They were never content, wanting *more than* and *different from* what they had. They were grumblers.

Me, too. I have this in common with the Israelites. We forgot to be grateful in the midst of transition.

For the first time this morning, I realized the Israelites were people also in transition. They left their home for a new one. They were going through unfamiliar territory. Being clearly led by God was good, but they didn't know exactly where they were going. They were on a journey, a prolonged camping trip through a wasteland. Packing, sorting, moving only to pack, sort and move again. For years.

Complaining increases in transition. I bristle in the unfamiliar. Complaints multiply, gratitude decreases. The less thankful I am, the easier it is to focus on myself and what I want or don't have. And the grumbling cycle continues.

At the first hint of a complaining attitude, I want to pause and remember to thank God. He is with me here, now, and always. I can choose to focus on who he is. I can recount his faithfulness through the years in every transition we've been through. I can remember his promises to lead and provide. He always knows everything. Though much is changing, and life feels unstable, he never changes. His presence with me provides stability through major life upheavals wherever I live.

May my heart transition from its tendency to grumble into one overflowing with gratitude.

Scripture

Rejoice always, pray continually, give thanks in all circumstances; for this is God's will for you in Christ Jesus. (1 Thess 5:16–18)

Questions

1. What does grumbling look like in your life?

2. How does transition affect you?

3. How can you develop a grateful heart?

Prayer

I am quick to grumble, slow to show gratitude. My focus slips to self, and I forget to look upward to you. My purposes rise to the forefront while yours take a backseat. When everything is unfamiliar, I long for the familiar. Forgive me for self-focused living and lack of God-focused gratitude. Thank you for guiding my steps, meeting my needs, and teaching me to value gratitude. Amen.

30
He Who Hesitates Isn't Always Lost

Almost everyone remembers an adult, or older sibling, who held their hand to help them. Maybe to help them cross a busy street. Or to help them jump into the deep end of the pool when they felt scared. Or to keep them from jumping in when they were reckless! When navigating a bustling crowd, holding hands helps us not get lost. Loved ones hold hands to share a connection, to show they aren't alone; they are facing life together.

I remember after a heavy rainstorm, my sister and I walked to our elementary school. I was in kindergarten. My attention wandered and I didn't notice a large puddle where the sidewalk dipped. I waded to the middle before I realized how deep the puddle was. The water was over my ankles. I stood there startled and wet. I don't know why I didn't walk out of the puddle. Hesitant to move forward or back, I stayed in the puddle and cried. My sister, heroic even in third grade, walked through the puddle, grabbed my hand, and led me out of the water. We continued our walk to school.

Holding hands. It can be a loving gesture to show you are fond of someone. Or a helpful gesture to those who need someone to steady them. Or help them escape a puddle! When someone faces danger, grabbing a hand can also be a life-saving push or pull.

In Genesis, the angels warned Lot about the coming destruction of his city and told him to leave quickly.

Lot hesitated. And when he did, the angels gripped his hand and the hands of those in his family and led them to safety.

> With the coming of dawn, the angels urged Lot, saying, "Hurry! Take your wife and your two daughters who are here, or you will be swept away when the city is punished."

> When he hesitated, the men grasped his hand and the hands of his wife and of his two daughters and led them safely out of the city, for the LORD was merciful to them.
>
> (Gen 19:15–16)

I love that the angels grabbed their hands. They didn't give up on him. They didn't try explaining again why they needed to move quickly. They didn't say he lost his chance and now he and his family were doomed. The angels grasped their hands and led them to safety.

We find several other passages that talk about God himself leading and protecting us by holding our hand.

> The LORD makes firm the steps
>
> of the one who delights in him;
>
> though he may stumble, he will not fall,
>
> for the LORD upholds him with his hand. (Ps 37:23–24)

> Peter got down out of the boat, walked on the water and came to Jesus. But when he saw the wind, he was afraid and, beginning to sink, cried out, "Lord, save me!" Immediately Jesus reached out his hand and caught him.
>
> (Matt 14:29–31a)

Whether we hesitate, stumble, or take our eyes off Jesus all is not lost. God is kind and merciful. He reaches out to grab our hands and leads us forward in our walk of faith.

His grip is sure, and he never lets go.

Scripture

> I call on you, my God, for you will answer me;
>
> turn your ear to me and hear my prayer.
>
> Show me the wonders of your great love,
>
> you who save by your right hand
>
> those who take refuge in you from their foes. (Ps 17:6–7)

Questions

1. What makes you hesitate to follow God's leading?

2. When have you experienced the blessing of someone holding your hand?

3. How can you come alongside others who need a helping hand?

Prayer

I thank you Father for holding my hand and never letting go. You never give up on me. When I hesitate to follow you, you don't throw up your hands in disgust and leave me on my own. You continue to hold my hand and remind me of your unshakeable grip. It is very reassuring to know I am never alone even when I show reluctance to follow you. Your faithfulness is magnificent. Amen.

31
A Pretzel Is Not a Strawberry and Other Lessons!

Someone asked me what some stressors are for people who serve across cultures. It led to a group of us brainstorming as we discussed challenges we face. I thought I'd share a few language and cultural mistakes we've experienced.

Language blunders

When we first moved to Spain, we needed to purchase an iron. At the store, I kept seeing the word "Plancha" in large letters. I didn't think to read the smaller print underneath the larger label. I hadn't heard of that brand before and told Don, "These 'Plancha' brand irons are all from the same company!" I kept looking for a more familiar brand like Braun or Philips. I eventually realized the small print labeled the brands. The big print identified the item. Plancha was the Spanish word for iron.

I discovered soft pretzels at our grocery store. I got one almost every week and enjoyed the special treat. But one day, I went to the bakery where they normally were and didn't find any. I walked all around the bakery in case they moved them somewhere else. I couldn't find them. I looked up how to say pretzel in Spanish. It is "pretzel." I thought this was going to be easy! I asked one of the bakers, "Dónde está el pretzel?" He looked at me and motioned me to follow him. So, I did. We left the bakery. We went to the fruit and vegetable section. He led me to the strawberries and handed me a carton of them. I was a bit surprised, but said, "Gracias" and waited until he left to put the strawberries back. I looked up strawberry in Spanish—"fresa." It sounds nothing like pretzel. I still don't know what went wrong.

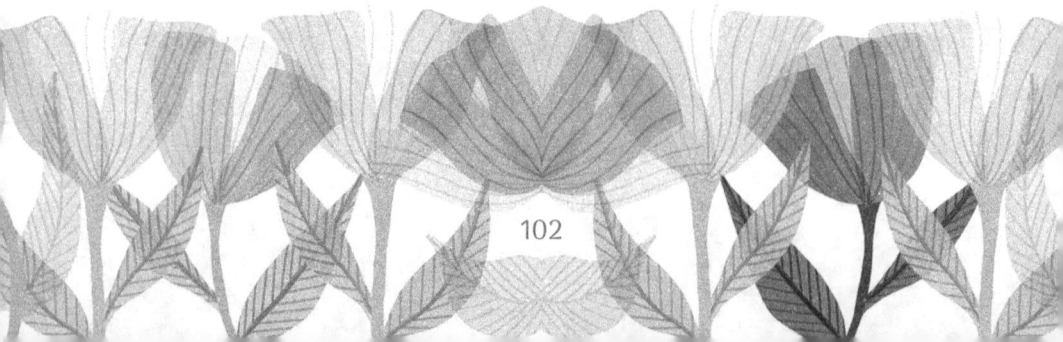

Cultural mishaps

Don went to an outreach event at a nearby beach. He didn't think to take any cash with him. In many public parking areas, unofficial parking guides are there to help. People pay the attendant a Euro, so he earns a little money as he offers help to find or leave a parking spot. But this time, Don had no change. He walked away without paying the Euro, not thinking it would be a problem. When he returned to the car, he saw that someone had broken the passenger sideview mirror. It dangled at an unnatural angle. Don was not trying to get out of paying the Euro but had to pay 150 Euro to repair the mirror. It is wise to have change on hand when parking to save money.

When waiting for the bus, people stand around or sit on seats at the bus stop. When it arrives, people know who got to the bus stop first and the order of all who came afterwards. This is the order for boarding the bus. Anywhere people are waiting, they are in a line. However, it isn't obvious. I need to know where I am at in the arrival order. Knowing my place in the "unline" helps me not offend others by jumping ahead of them.

Conclusion

None of these adjustments are super difficult in and of themselves. It makes me feel a little silly that there is so much I don't know. But the only way to learn some cultural norms is by making mistakes. And we make a lot of mistakes, especially in the first few years. The learning curve is steep. It can feel overwhelming. We may start out confident—we know our own culture and language. We go serve in a country where we don't know much about either of those. Little children may ask us, "Why do you speak like a baby?" How humbling!

We know, though, that humility is good. Adapting is important. We want to share Good News with others—a worthy goal that merits every effort.

Progress may be slow, but we learn to celebrate the small victories. I now know where to find pretzels. Whenever I get one, I celebrate finding it and not a strawberry!

Scripture

Therefore, my dear brothers and sisters, stand firm. Let nothing move you. Always give yourselves fully to the work of the Lord, because you know that your labor in the Lord is not in vain. (1 Cor 15:58)

Questions

1. What is your funniest language blunder?

2. How has God developed humility in your life?

3. How would you encourage a new missionary who felt discouraged?

Prayer

There is so much to learn in a new culture. When I learn, I am encouraged. When I mess up, I feel like going home because I'm not sure I'll ever learn all I need to know. Thank you that my efforts are worthwhile. Thank you for the privilege to learn another language, to have the opportunity to share the gospel through deed and word. Continue to help me work hard and remain steadfast for your glory. Amen.

32
Waiting on the Who, Not the What

I recently listened to a podcast based on the book, *The Ruthless Elimination of Hurry*,[1] by John Mark Comer. For several of the episodes I increased the video speed to 1.5 because of my busy day and upcoming appointments. I'm pretty sure that is *not* what the author of that book intended.

Waiting is one of my least favorite things to do. It highlights uncertainty and my lack of control over life events and outcomes. Waiting confirms to me that my timing and God's are different. I am in a rush. He isn't. Time is critical to me. He lives beyond it. The Lord uses time for his purposes and is always wisely in charge of "when."

When a loved one is sick, I presume we should know something definite *soon*. I think, "At the next doctor's appointment, we will know what it is and what we should do." But that appointment comes and goes. We find out we need to wait for yet another test and a different medical appointment.

I'm impatient in other spheres of life, too. When seeking to make a wise decision, I need to get some vital piece of information. Who knew that needed information could prove so hard to find? And even when found, wise next steps still may not be clear.

For those of us in cross-cultural ministry, we complete visa application forms. We accumulate all the necessary documents only to find out we need another form. Or we got the wrong one. Or the date expired. We raise support and wait for the needed amount. We are anxious to go but can't until the timing, approvals, and support coincide. Once we get to our country of service, we study language and learn about our new culture.

---

1 John Mark Comer, *The Ruthless Elimination of Hurry* (Colorado Springs: WaterBrook, 2019).

We anticipate the day we can conjugate verbs and understand what people say. It takes time to learn how to communicate in a new language.

Waiting. It doesn't sound hard. We grow up waiting and get lots of practice. We wait for the cookies to bake, recess to come, the school year to end and summer vacation to start. As we get older, we gain more experience waiting. We fill out college applications and wait. We go to job interviews and wait to hear if we get it. We save money to buy a house. None of those things come immediately, and some not at all.

So, why doesn't waiting become easier for me when I've had practice? This month I am pretty sure I've discovered why.

Normally, I wait for what I need. I look to that next medical appointment to find out what we need to know. Or the next government office when we discover what other documents we need. My expectations and hope focus on what I need or where I need to go to find answers. Once I get what I need, I am ready to move on until the next thing.

Rather than anxiously wait for "the what" I need, I must shift my focus to "the Who" I need. No longer do I want my focus to be on the *what*, but the *Who*.

I need to place my hope and expectation on my heavenly Father and not the next appointment. To wait on my Rock and Refuge is a subtle, but life changing, shift. I'm still working out how to put this into practice. But for now, each day I remind myself I am waiting on the Lord, my creator and sustainer. Not the doctor. Not a government official. Not another person or event, but God Almighty himself.

Scripture confirms that he is to be where I focus as I wait. The psalmist wrote:

> Wait for the LORD; be strong and take heart and wait for the LORD. (Ps 27:14)

> I wait for the LORD, my whole being waits, and in his word
> I put my hope. (Ps 130:5)

Waiting for the Lord involves trusting him in the uncertainty. We have confidence in his purposes, his timing, his presence with us—every day.

While I wait for the who, the what will follow in his perfect timing and my soul finds rest in the waiting.

Scripture

We wait in hope for the LORD;
> he is our help and our shield.
In him our hearts rejoice,
> for we trust in his holy name.
May your unfailing love be with us, LORD,
> even as we put our hope in you. (Ps 33:20–23)

Questions

1. What are the main differences in waiting for the who and waiting for the what?

2. What is your normal way of dealing with uncertainty?

3. How does a person wait well for the Lord?

Prayer

We have so much instantly at our disposal. Instant pots for quick meals in the kitchen. Google with everything we want to know at the click of a link. I think I have it easier than younger people because I remember having to wait longer for things. But maybe it's harder because I do remember and didn't like waiting then! I get used to quick fixes and I get anxious when I must wait longer than I think I should. Remove the anxiety that tries to take over and makes me fret. Empower me to wait in hope because you are my Lord. Amen.

33
More Than Human Hope

"I hope you have a nice trip." "I hope this cake is tasty." "I hope I win this game."

Hope seems like a weak word to me. Hearing "I hope you feel better soon," spoken with a sigh, doesn't inspire confidence. When I say, "I hope it works out," I don't always sense that it will. I watch a football game and *hope* the receiver catches the quarterback's pass. When he doesn't, I'm disappointed. Especially if it is a team I am rooting for. When he does catch it, I'm thrilled. But hope doesn't seem to affect the outcome. I sometimes view hope as a wish or strong desire. Sometimes it comes true. Often it doesn't. There are no guarantees, but I hope.

I'm not sure why Paul includes hope as one of the big three remaining virtues in 1 Corinthians 13—faith, hope and love. I understand faith is vital. Love is crucial. But hope?

When I hope something, I am never sure about the outcome. I try to have a bit of optimism, but hope appears fragile. My view of hope feels more like a cross-your-fingers-and-hope-but-it-might-not-happen kind of wish. How does this wishful thinking fit in with abiding faith and love?

Reading through the New Testament I see a human kind of hope. Herod hoped to see Jesus perform a miracle (Luke 23:8). Paul hoped to go see Timothy (1 Tim 3:14) and Philemon (Phlm 1:22). So, there is hope, an expectancy that something will come about. We devise a plan or face a challenge and hope for a desired outcome. What will happen isn't certain, but we hope.

Paul mentions a different kind of hope in 1 Corinthians 15. He starts off by writing how important Jesus's resurrection is. Because of God's power, we know the dead are resurrected. There is hope after death. And then he contrasts that kind of hopeful trust with human hopes. He wrote,

"If I fought wild beasts in Ephesus *with no more than human hopes*, what have I gained? If the dead are not raised, 'Let us eat and drink, for tomorrow we die'" (15:32, emphasis mine). If there is nothing beyond human hope, then let's live for today because nothing is certain.

Yet, Paul had a hope beyond human standards. Eternal hope enabled him to endure challenges and suffering. Everlasting hope is stronger, a more definite hope with an assured eternal outcome. Paul knew God was with him, at work in and through him. Heaven was certain. Because of his relationship with Jesus, he had confidence in the power of God. This eternal hope gave him assurance of an eternal purpose through temporary hardships.

Now I see that hope has two facets. One is human hope. Having human hope is good and normal. "I hope you read my blog. I hope we have a nice holiday. I hope my family stays healthy." I hope it will happen. If not, it will still be okay because I can trust that my heavenly Father has a different and better plan.

In contrast, eternal hope is certain. Powerful. Unrelenting. Supernatural. This hope has its foundation in the power of God. This kind of hope can make the dead come alive and is confident of eternal life in the kingdom of God. Because Jesus rose from the dead and all power belongs to God, we have hope knowing he will never let us down.

This isn't the human type of hope—it is the eternal kind. God not only gives this hope as we trust him, but he gives the power to live overflowing with hope.

Therefore, I hope for good now and the eternal good to come, knowing both are in God's powerful hands.

Scripture

May the God of hope fill you with all joy and peace as you trust in him, so that you may overflow with hope by the power of the Holy Spirit. (Rom 15:13)

Questions

1. How would you describe overflowing with hope?

2. What feels hopeless to you now?

3. What does it mean knowing that God is "the God of hope"?

Prayer

I admit that hope doesn't overflow in my life. When life feels full, what overflows is worry, fear, plans, and remedies for when things go wrong. Forgive me. May I trust you so fully, that when opportunities to trust you come my way, hope is what spills out. This can only happen with your power. I ask that I would be filled with your Spirit. May joy, peace and hope characterize my life especially in the middle of what feels impossible. Amen.

34
Sometimes I Miss Me

I look in the mirror and see the same person looking back at me wherever I am. I enjoy interacting with people. I love humor and am usually friendly. I am an extrovert. Whether overseas or in my home country, I am me.

But it isn't that simple. Landing at the airport for our first term more than thirty-seven years ago, I noticed a change. I wasn't comfortable. I didn't know the language or customs of our host country. I didn't know where places were and if I found them, I didn't know what to do once I got there! I felt out of place. Obviously foreign. And it felt like my personality shifted.

Experts say personalities don't change. If you are born an extrovert, you will stay an extrovert. I was still an extrovert. But not in the same way. I felt like a paler version of myself.

I wanted to chat with people but couldn't. I wanted to be friendly but wasn't sure how to do that in the new culture. I watched groups of friends interacting and wanted to join in. But I was an outsider. I didn't fit. And even if they invited me to join them, conversations were stilted. I felt our differences keenly. After a while I became used to the new me. A little quieter. Less talkative. I didn't laugh as freely. I was still me, but not quite.

When we don't learn the language well or work hard to adapt to our host culture, it is easy to get stuck there. At the "not quite me."

In our first home overseas, I studied the language and learned about the culture. In time, I became more like the old me. I made friends. I learned to tell jokes. I loved telling old jokes in a new language to new friends who hadn't heard them before! I sat in groups and felt more and more comfortable. I didn't look the same as my new friends. I had an accent. But they were patient with me. They were warm, loving, and kind. We could chat and build friendships. I started to fit.

I felt more like me. Not quite, but close enough that I recognized myself.

Then we went back to the US on home assignment, and I discovered the real me again. It was like slipping back into a comfortable pair of jeans after wearing something that didn't fit quite right. I felt more at home. It was easier to talk with people. And I did so. In lines, on the street, at the mall—because I could! Confident that we would be able to understand each other, I chatted to people I knew and people I didn't. It felt wonderful. No caution. I needed no extra brainpower to translate words or conjugate verbs.

Through the years I have become more comfortable with the two me's. I am fairly secure in both versions. One is more comfortable, but the other has become familiar. We are the same me. But living in a different culture with a different language does influence how I act and who I sense that I am. And that's OK.

For both of me.

Scripture

> **For you created my inmost being;**
> **you knit me together in my mother's womb.**
> **I praise you because I am fearfully and wonderfully made;**
> **your works are wonderful,**
> **I know that full well. (Ps 139:13–14)**

Questions

1. What differences have you seen in your personality in your new culture?

2. How does knowing God made you and knows you intimately help you as you adapt to where you live?

3. How else has your move across cultures changed you?

Prayer

You know me better than I know myself, Lord. You see the depths of my soul and the hidden places of which I am yet unaware. You see the real me. You see the tension I feel when I try to be me in new places. I feel insecure, a bit lost. It is hard when no one really knows me. Thank you for reminding me that you made me, know me, and treasure me. There is nothing hidden from you that will scare you away or make you love me less. I am known by you and that makes all the difference. Amen.

35
Seeking Wisdom

After Solomon became king, God told him to ask for whatever he wanted so that God could give it to him (2 Chron 1).

What might we have asked for? Maybe money enough to never have to worry? Maybe a long and healthy life? Success? Most of the ideas that pop up first in my mind focus on me and what would make my life better and easier. Solomon asked for wisdom and knowledge to lead his people well. He knew it was going to be hard, and knew he needed to know more for his kingdom to prosper.

What made him ask for wisdom above all else he could have asked for?

Well, his dad, King David, planted the seed for his request when Solomon was a little boy. He wrote Proverbs and shared wisdom for his son (and any other sons who would read them). Solomon mentioned how his father influenced him:

> When I was a son to my father,
>   Tender and the only son in the sight of my mother,
> Then he taught me and said to me,
>   "Let your heart hold fast my words;
>   Keep my commandments and live;
> Acquire wisdom! Acquire understanding!"
>   (Prov 4:3–5a, NASB)

Proverbs 4 emphasizes the importance of gaining wisdom. Solomon's regard for wisdom started when his father, King David, taught him how important it was (Prov 4:7).

As I made this connection between what he learned as a child and his decisions as an adult, I thought of two facts. Two realities we already know, but sometimes forget in the day-to-day busyness of living.

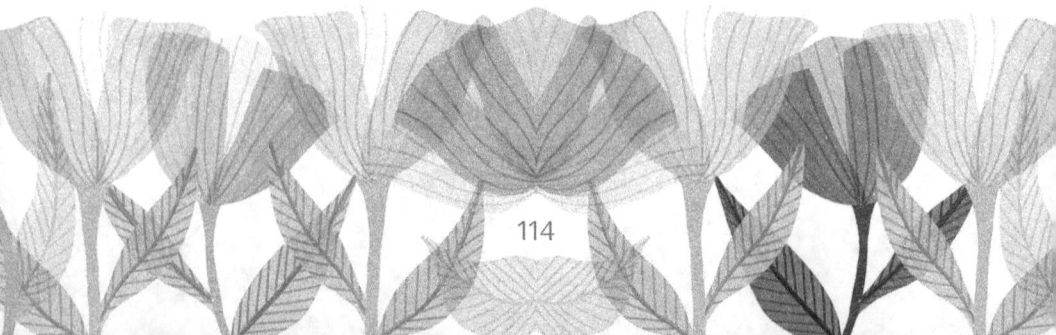

First, parents have a tremendous responsibility and privilege to teach their children. About life. God. Responsibility. The importance of wisdom. The foundation parents lay influences future generations. As parents are aware of this huge undertaking, they may feel overwhelmed. Parenting, maybe more than any other role we have, makes us aware of how much wisdom we need. Raising little humans well is not easy!

Which leads to my second point. The invitation to acquire wisdom continues. James wrote, "If any of you lacks wisdom, you should ask God, who gives generously to all without finding fault, and it will be given to you" (Jas 1:5). When we ask God for wisdom, he liberally gives it. This wisdom God gives includes what we need in parenting. But it is also for any and every arena in life.

I need wisdom in decision making. Ministry direction. Relationship issues. Scheduling my day. Any challenge that comes my way, when I know I am in over my head—may I be wise enough to ask my heavenly Father for wisdom. He isn't stingy with it and loves to give it to those who ask.

Scripture

Choose my instruction instead of silver,
> **knowledge rather than choice gold,**

for wisdom is more precious than rubies,
> **and nothing you desire can compare with her.**

"I, wisdom, dwell together with prudence;
> **I possess knowledge and discretion."** (Prov 8:10–12)

Questions

1. How do you gain wisdom?

2. What situation are you in which highlights your need for wisdom?

3. How can you influence children to value wisdom as they grow?

Prayer

I need wisdom today. You invite me to come to you and ask for it. You give it liberally and you don't find fault with us for asking. It is the wise thing to do! Thank you for your generosity. You know all things. You always know what is best. I look to you and refuse to look to my own insight when I need yours. Amen.

36
When God Says You're Old— You Must Be!

I found a new rest-of-my-life theme verse. "When Joshua had grown old, the LORD said to him, "You are now very old, and there are still very large areas of land to be taken over'" (Josh 13:1).

Joshua was getting older and just in case he didn't realize it, God reminded him: "You are now very old." God always speaks truth. If God thought Joshua was old, he was old!

But the reason this verse resonates with me is the next part after acknowledging Joshua's age. "There are still very large areas of land to be taken over." Joshua still had more to do!

No one ever gets so old that they have nothing else to do. God always has a plan for us and a part for us to play in doing his will.

Joshua's friend, Caleb, was forty when he spied out the land. And forty-five years later he says:

> I am still as strong today as the day Moses sent me out; I'm just as vigorous to go out to battle now as I was then. Now give me this hill country that the LORD promised me that day. You yourself heard then that the Anakites were there and their cities were large and fortified, but, the LORD helping me, I will drive them out just as he said. (Josh 14:11–12)

Caleb was eighty-five and looking at the next thing. Ready to battle and take on the hill country, he didn't choose the easy. He chose the hard. I am not as old as Joshua or Caleb, but I am getting older!

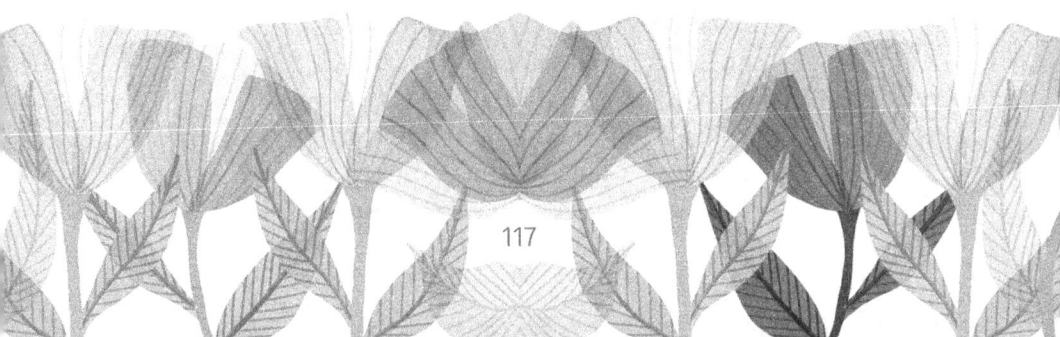

Some translations call the hill country a mountain. I like that image and ask myself, "What is another mountain that I could tackle?" It would be easy to want to stay at ground level. It seems less dangerous here. Mountains look high. Foreboding. But I've learned that one of the dangers of growing older is plateauing. We can become too easily satisfied with what *was* and not excited enough about what *could be*. I don't want to plateau—fade away as life goes on and opportunities abound. That would be living as though life is finished when there is still more race to run.

And so, I look for another mountain. I might not scale it as quickly as I once did. I could stumble. I may need to take a few breathers. To others it might not even look like a mountain. It doesn't matter. I am asking God for more mountains.

I see that Caleb was moving forward because he knew the promises of God and that the Lord would be helping him. I, too, can rely on the promises of God and I know that the Lord will help me. God has a purpose for me to fulfill until he calls me home.

And so, what are the strengths God has given me? Where are the needs that stir my soul? What would God have me do? What is my next mountain? How will I know?

Joshua and Caleb knew because they followed the Lord wholeheartedly (Num 32:12). They were ready for the next mountain because they knew God. They trusted him and his promises. These two men lived out their faith—fervently. I want to age with an audacious, faith-inspired life like Joshua and Caleb.

Joshua died when he was 110 years old. They buried him in the hill country. It isn't clear when Caleb died or where he was buried, but I would suggest they also buried him in the hill country, on higher ground. Maybe that last mountain he conquered? No matter how old we are, each of us can look to the Lord and ask, "What is my next mountain?"

Scripture

Listen to me, you descendants of Jacob,
    all the remnant of the people of Israel,
you whom I have upheld since your birth,
    and have carried since you were born.
Even to your old age and gray hairs
    I am he, I am he who will sustain you.
I have made you and I will carry you;
    I will sustain you and I will rescue you. (Isa 46:3–4)

Questions

1. What would plateauing look like for you?

2. What comforts draw you toward complacency? What are the dangers of it?

3. What could be your next mountain?

Prayer

Give me another mountain, Lord. May I not be content with the status quo. I have the privilege of looking back over my life and seeing your faithfulness. At those times I fought fear and stepped out, you met me there. The impossible loomed large before my eyes and you brought me through. Help me not to grow too comfortable but to keep my eyes on you. Lead me to the next mountain for your glory. Amen.

37

What Would I Tell My Younger Me Starting My First Term Overseas?

It takes time to adjust. Don't rush the process. The first term is where we focus on learning. Be ready to make mistakes. Embrace them. Mistakes teach us. When you take that first language test and you miss every single question, don't panic. Be prepared to study more and plan more visits—as much as you can with four kids while trying to stay sane. Your ministry to your family and in your new community are both valuable investments of time. Work hard. Work wisely. Worry less. Pray more. You are doing fine. It is slow going and that is OK. You are learning to endure by enduring—a lesson you will need far into the future!

Maintain your sense of humor. Don't waste time feeling foolish. Laugh at your mistakes. When you ask the little girl in your new language, what her doll's name is and she says, "lisa." You will learn that word it is not a name like it is in America. It means, "Not yet." She will not have named her doll yet and she will look at you strangely when you say that Lisa is a beautiful name. Everyone makes mistakes. It takes time for everyone to learn and adjust. Nothing is simple. Life takes more time. Everything moves more slowly. Relax.

You will learn more than language! You are not only learning language and culture, but you are also learning about yourself and God. Your deepest spiritual lessons will come in the middle of your deepest struggles. You will feel like you are in over your head. You are. You will not understand what people are saying. You will feel lost. You will feel needy. You will get to know God in entirely new ways while seeing yourself at your weakest.

These are life-changing lessons that will spur you to rely more and more on the Lord. This is good. It is good to know your weakness and imperative to know God's strength. God will meet you where you are and be your rock in the sea of bewilderment. He uses these times of trouble to build maturity and endurance into your life.

Be grateful for how God has gifted you. For a while you are not going to feel needed. You will wonder why in the world you are there. You won't think your gifts seem important for the ministry at first. Others' gifts will seem more vital. You will be tempted to envy them and how God is using them. Take your eyes off others and keep them on Jesus. Be patient. Develop the gifts you have. Trust God in his giving of gifts and timing of you being where you are. Look for opportunities to develop and grow. Be faithful. Your gifts are important. Others' gifts are important, too. Rejoice in others' gifts and pray for blessings on them. We serve our Lord together.

Hang in there. There will be ups and downs. Closed doors and open doors. You think you're going to stay in one place, but you will end up moving quite a few times. Trust God through each transition. You will come to discover God's faithfulness more and more. It can be an exhilarating journey at times and boring at others. Be steadfast in both. Cling to the Lord. Stay in the word. Don't stop learning. Repent when convicted (don't rationalize or put it off as you sometimes do!). Stay the course.

Know God's plan is good. He will see you through as you walk by faith. One day you will look back in amazement at all God has done. You will experience the Lord's goodness and faithfulness through your hardest moments. You will never be alone but always in his hands.

What a journey you will have! Hang on and trust Jesus.

Scripture

> Consider it pure joy, my brothers and sisters, whenever you face trials of many kinds, because you know that the testing of your faith produces perseverance. Let perseverance finish its work so that you may be mature and complete, not lacking anything. (Jas 1:2–4)

Questions

1. What would you write in a letter to your younger self? (Write it!)

2. What have been some ups and downs you've experienced?

3. How have you experienced God's faithfulness recently?

Prayer

I thank you, Father, for knowing me. You guide me. You have a good plan for me. I've learned so much through the years because you used events in my life to teach me. Your Holy Spirit was at work when I didn't even know. I thought I was on my own, working through hardships and I look back and see I was never alone. You have been faithful, and I remain grateful. Amen.

38
Gideon and "Just One Earring"

Sometimes I admire Gideon. Other times I don't understand him. At times he disappoints me.

We read about Gideon in Judges 6–8. He is a bit fearful, not super trusting, but also teachable. He had questions and recognized he was weak. Yet when God told him to "Go in the strength that you have" (Judg 6:14), he went. God used Gideon in mighty ways to deliver his people and ultimately bring glory to God's name. Hebrews 11:32 mentions him as one of the heroes of the faith.

As Gideon led in battle, with God's strength, they conquered their enemies. As a result, the people wanted him and his sons after him to lead them. I love Gideon's response after hearing their request for him to rule:

> But Gideon told them, "I will not rule over you, nor will my son rule over you. The LORD will rule over you."
> (Judg 8:23)

I wish the story ended there. He honored God. He knew and let his people know that the Lord is the best ruler. But then it goes downhill because of his one small request:

> And he said, "I do have one request, that each of you give me an earring from your share of the plunder."
> (Judg 8:24a)

One earring.

That doesn't sound that bad as a thank you for his leadership—a way to reward him for all his hard work and efforts. But one earring per person added up to a lot of gold earrings! Let's see what happened after that:

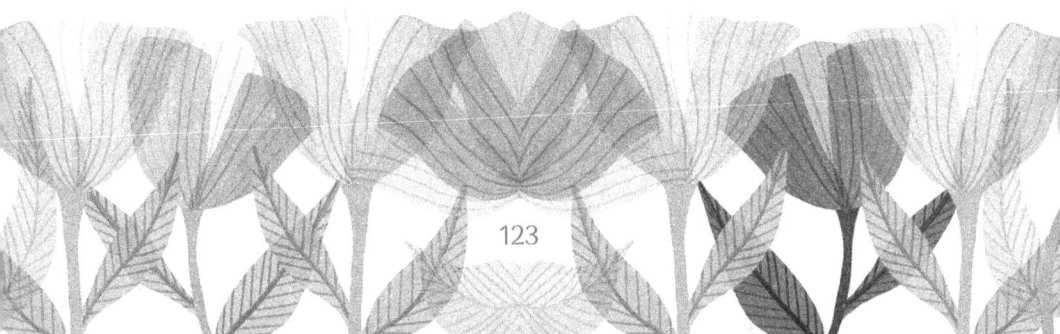

> They answered, "We'll be glad to give them." So they spread out a garment, and each of them threw a ring from his plunder onto it. The weight of the gold rings he asked for came to seventeen hundred shekels, not counting the ornaments, the pendants and the purple garments worn by the kings of Midian or the chains that were on their camels' necks. Gideon made the gold into an ephod, which he placed in Ophrah, his town. All Israel prostituted themselves by worshiping it there, and it became a snare to Gideon and his family. (Judg 8:25–27)

One earring from each person added up to 1,700 shekels, which is between 50 to 70 pounds of gold! (That wasn't counting the rest of the plunder that Gideon had.) He used the gold to make an ephod. An ephod is a priestly garment, like an apron. He placed it in his hometown, and it became something people worshiped. Did he wear it, thus proclaiming himself a priest? Was he seeking to lead the people after all his protestation to the contrary? It is hard to figure out from the text exactly what happened. But what is clear is that it not only led Israel into false worship but became a snare to Gideon. And his family.

The downfall began with one earring.

What might be my "one earring"? Could it be a hidden sin that is easy to rationalize—until I can no longer hide it? Maybe nursing a little bitterness in my heart against a teammate? Yet, that bitterness can easily turn into broken relationships. I can skip one morning of prayer and time with God. But one skip can easily turn into skipping a week, a month and then my time with God becomes a long-lost memory. Allowing one little worry can become a heartful of anxiety.

I want to be on my guard. If I'm not, my "one little earring" could turn into a giant snare for me—and my family! Ripple effects could go further, influencing others in negative ways. My one slip into faithlessness could disillusion others. Distract them from the one true God and encourage idolatry. All because I looked for and welcomed one seemingly insignificant thing.

May the Lord rule over me.

No earrings requested.

Scripture

Dear friends, I urge you, as foreigners and exiles, to abstain from sinful desires, which wage war against your soul. Live such good lives among the pagans that, though they accuse you of doing wrong, they may see your good deeds and glorify God on the day he visits us.

(1 Pet 2:11–12)

Questions

1. What have been some sins that are easy for you to rationalize?

2. What are some spiritual disciplines that help you in your war against sin?

3. What parts of Gideon's story resonate with you? (Judg 6–8)

Prayer

By your power may I abstain from sinful desires that embattle my soul. It is easy to accept them as weaknesses or convince myself it isn't so bad. Others deal with far worse sins. May I listen to your voice, be quick to repent, and sincere in following your lead in my life. Amen.

39
Therefore, We Will Not Fear

I was reading Psalm 46 and noticed these words in verse 2: "Therefore we will not fear." The first verse tells me why I need not fear. "God is our refuge and strength, an ever-present help in trouble." God is never absent—there is never a time when God isn't present. He is always available to be our refuge. There is never a time when God lacks strength. He is always all-powerful. Because God is who he says he is, I don't have to be afraid no matter what is happening around me.

The verses that come after "Therefore we will not fear" list a lot of *even thoughs*. Even though the earth gives way, the mountains fall into the sea, the seas roar and foam, the mountains quake. These would normally cause me to not only be afraid but to panic! What makes it so terrifying? I have no control over nature and disasters that occur. It stresses me just thinking about all that would happen if the stability I've known were to go unpredictably wild. Instability scares me.

The psalmist also mentions nations being in an uproar and kingdoms falling. I also have no control over national tensions and political divides. I have no influence over world powers or what international leaders decide to do. Wars. Riots. Volatility. These all happen outside of what I can personally do to control the process or outcomes. I have no power over a pandemic or responses to it.

Beyond natural disasters and global troubles, there are my personal quaking mountains. What was once familiar isn't the familiar anymore. Transitions or preparing for them has become normal. My aging body experiences more aches and pains. I have less energy and more limitations. Saying earthly goodbyes is more commonplace. All these things tend to make me feel unsettled. Insecure.

Fear is my first response to events outside of my comfort zone, things that highlight my lack of control. I read the news. I hear different perspectives about what should or shouldn't be done. Strife occurs within the church and outside of it. Changes occur rapidly. Pervasive social media is relentless in opinions, likes, and dislikes.

When fear tries to make its home in my soul, this psalm brings me back to truth. No matter what is happening all around me or within me, God is still God. I need not fear.

Frantically trying to think of how to solve everything, and then realizing that I can't, leads me to despair. Worrying about worst-case scenarios doesn't help. Fretting about what might happen to me and my loved ones isn't productive. None of this solves anything! It urges me to carry burdens that aren't mine to bear.

In Psalm 46:10, the psalmist concludes with what we need to do. Even considering all the out-of-our-control happenings in the world, he writes, "Be still and know that I am God."

Because God is who he says he is. Because he is our refuge and strength. Because he is an ever-present help in trouble. Therefore, we will not fear.

No matter what.

We can be still and know that he is God. Our refuge. Fortress. The Lord Almighty. He is with us.

Scripture

> But you, LORD, are a shield around me,
>   my glory, the One who lifts my head high.
> I call out to the LORD,
>   and he answers me from his holy mountain.
> I lie down and sleep;
>   I wake again because the LORD sustains me.
> I will not fear though tens of thousands
>   assail me on every side. (Ps 3:3–6)

Questions

1. What are a few of your existing fears?

2. What does it look like to be still?

3. How are current events influencing your life of faith?

Prayer

I confess that fear is a huge issue for me. It is almost always my first response to anything new, uncertain, or risky. I forget that you are all powerful, and I think I have only my own strength and wisdom to see me through. I'm sorry. May I remember first and foremost that you are God, you love me and I can rest secure in you. Amen.

40
My Whiny Voice Within

"But I don't want to go back overseas!" This is what my inner whiny voice is saying.

We have one more month left of our five-month home assignment. And I find myself not wanting to get back on the plane.

These feelings are familiar. We've been in cross-cultural ministry a long time, and I know this is normal. Getting back on the plane is always hard. My body goes and my heart catches up a few days, or weeks, later. I know once we get resettled and into the ministry where God has called us, we will be glad.

But it is still hard.

These past few months I have thoroughly enjoyed:

- Unrushed conversations with family.
- Tea parties, birthday celebrations, and baseball games with grandchildren.
- Connecting with old friends.
- Conversing in English with strangers.
- Watching Andy Griffith with my dad.
- Eating favorite foods.
- Having face-to-face time with loved ones.
- Being my normally extrovertish self with no cultural or language barriers.

I'm going to miss these things. I've already started missing loved ones, and I haven't even left yet!

Part of our furlough has been a sabbatical. We've been able to rest. We felt refreshed by getting away. Our souls are renewed. We've gained fresh vision. It's been beneficial.

We've also been raising needed support. We report to churches who love us and give so that we can serve in ministry. Communicating to churches about what we've been doing and how we've been serving has been good for them and us. Sometimes inside of me I can feel pressure and insecurity. What if I'm not doing enough, fruitful enough, or spiritual enough? But, as we share our joys, sorrows, successes, and challenges, churches listen. And care. They have responded with kind encouragement to keep pressing on.

We also spend time with friends who support us financially and in prayer. Being with people who show interest in our lives and our ministry is affirming. But the focus isn't just us and our role. It is really about the great commission. We all desire to see the nations know about salvation found only in Jesus.

Our calling is important. Looking to do God's will and serve his purposes for us is imperative.

And costly.

So, I plan to get on the plane. It will hurt. I will cry. But my heart will catch up with me soon. And I know I will once again thrive in life and ministry there.

My whiny voice will subside, and gratitude will take its place. I can be grateful for the time here and the new memories I can now cherish. I can be thankful for the opportunity to play my small part in the great commission.

I can tell my whiny voice to be quiet as I remember the privilege to serve wherever God leads.

Scripture

> **Suppose one of you has a servant plowing or looking after the sheep. Will he say to the servant when he comes in from the field, "Come along now and sit down to eat"? Won't he rather say, "Prepare my supper, get yourself ready and wait on me while I eat and drink; after that you may eat and drink"? Will he thank the servant because he did what he was told to do? So you also, when you have done everything you were told to do, should say, "We are unworthy servants; we have only done our duty." (Luke 17:7–10)**

Questions

1. What do you enjoy in your home country that makes it hard to leave?

2. What helps you say goodbye well?

3. How has God been faithful to you in the past when you returned with broken hearts?

Prayer

Sometimes this commission to cross-cultural ministry is painful. Sometimes I resent all the goodbyes, the moves, and the constant missing of what once was. Yet, I know you are worthy of any sacrifice. Your kingdom is eternal and my life here is so short. May I live with eternity in view and serve your purposes, not my own. I ask for strength, grace, and hope as I navigate what is hard with an eye toward what is glorious. Amen.

41
Parenting Seemed Easy, Until I Had Kids!

When my children were little, I was listening to a talk about being a good parent. I was in the kitchen and the kids were playing in another room. Something must have triggered the hunger bug in all of them! All four came clamoring into the kitchen for a snack. I remember snapping at them, "Be quiet! I am busy learning how to be a better mom!"

Parenting is one of the hardest jobs on the planet! Not only are we caring, nurturing, training, loving, feeding, and clothing little people, we are also helping them grow up into mature, responsible, God-loving big people. At times it can feel overwhelming. Add living and serving cross-culturally to the mix and overwhelming seems too small of a descriptor!

Just when I would think I had parenting down, reality would hit. I remember listening to a radio program about keeping children safe. The speaker spoke about child proofing your house. We were to keep all poisonous cleaning supplies out of kids' reach. Well of course, I thought, I knew that. I was in the middle of congratulating myself when my toddler came into the kitchen. He was holding a can of cleanser in one hand and a fine layer of powder dusting his clothes. In a flash my self-congratulations transformed into self-criticism! I had forgotten to put the cleanser away after cleaning the bathroom. I felt awful.

Of course, there are any number of difficult things to deal with as parents. Kids who struggle, get sick, and need help. They can face physical, emotional, and spiritual struggles. As parents we face those with them!

When challenges seemed insurmountable and I felt unable to help my children, I began scouring through the gospels to read about other parents who needed help. They brought their children to Jesus and asked him to intervene. They asked for his blessing. They asked for healing. Jesus never turned them away. He never said, "Oh my, I don't know what to do!" Praying for our children, bringing them to Jesus, is something all parents can do. It is the best thing we can do. And we do so boldly, knowing Jesus not only loves our kids, but he is also limitless in his power to help!

I invite you to look at the following passages. Note the circumstances, what the child needed, what the parents did, and how Jesus responded:

- Matthew 9:18–26; Mark 5:21–43; Luke 8:40–56 (Jairus's daughter)
- Matthew 17:14–21; Mark 9:14–29; Luke 9:37–43 (Jesus heals boy with demon)
- Matthew 19:13–15; Mark 10:13–16; Luke 18:15–17 (Asking Jesus to bless kids)
- Matthew 20:20–28 (Mother of James and John)
- Mark 7:24–30; Matthew 15:21–28 (Syrophoenician woman's daughter)
- Luke 7:11–17 (Widow's son, where Jesus intervenes without her asking!)
- John 4:46–54 (A royal official's son)

As parents, we are never hopeless. No situation is too hard for God. No child is beyond the reach of our Savior. We can always bring our children to Jesus. We pray for them and seek his blessing for them as well as his help for the challenges they are facing.

Though my children are now adults, I still bring them to Jesus. And now, I also bring my grandchildren. There is no greater thing I can do, as a mother and grandmother, than to pray for my children and these children born to them. Jesus always welcomes children … and those who bring them to him.

Scripture

> Then people brought little children to Jesus for him to place his hands on them and pray for them. But the disciples rebuked them.
>
> Jesus said, "Let the little children come to me, and do not hinder them, for the kingdom of heaven belongs to such as these." When he had placed his hands on them, he went on from there. (Matt 19:13–15)

Questions

1. Why would the disciples rebuke people for bringing children to Jesus?

2. What stages are the hardest stages in life for kids?

3. In what ways do you pray for the children in your life?

Prayer

I thank you for the invitation to come to you in prayer. You never turn me away. You always hear. You know the burdens I carry and how overwhelmed I feel when I look at the task of influencing children for you. Would you work where I cannot? Will you touch hearts where I can only see behavior? Will you work in grace and might for your glory in all our lives? Amen.

42
Healing Is a Process, Not an Event

When using the word "healing" in this chapter's title, I don't mean only physical recuperation from broken bones. Healing includes emotional refueling when exhausted and mental recovery after fatigue. It even entails spiritual renewal after an especially dry season. Of course, sometimes God works a miracle and instantly heals and renews. It seems, though, that he often likes to use time to cultivate our growth and dependence on him as we wait in faith.

Everything, almost always, takes longer than we anticipated. Visa renewals, language learning, cultural adaptation, deepening team relationships, all take time. Longer than we expect. A lot longer than we hoped.

My friend Judi made a comment about pregnancy. She said when a woman finds out she is pregnant she doesn't have a full-term baby right away. It takes nine months, and that last month can sometimes feel like forever! Women can use those nine months to prepare. Read books. Decorate a nursery. Have health checkups. Interview and watch other moms. Stockpile diapers and wipes.

When healing, we have several different options. We can moan, groan, and complain at how long it is taking. I've tried this and it isn't helpful. It is easier for me to see how far I need to go rather than how far I've come. I tend to focus on what I can't do rather than what I can do once again.

Or I can acknowledge the discomfort—and yet be thankful for progress. I can rejoice that pain brings gain. I know that recovery comes through the aches and discomfort. Without the short-term hurt there can be no long-term strength. I can't discount or ignore the pain because it really does ache. However, I can also choose to keep moving forward. Keep exercising. Keep trusting that healing is coming.

We need time in almost all areas of healing, usually more than we anticipate. Grief comes in waves and sometimes tsunamis. Comfort weaves in and out through the storms. Exhaustion depletes and devastates, and it usually happens over time. Why would healing happen in an instant? Recuperating requires lots of rest, sleep, and more rest. Feeling emotionally drained, our tanks empty, leaves us with little energy or desire for much needed help.

I have come to look at the time it takes to heal as a gift from God. It is in the waiting that our walk of faith deepens. We find we can depend on God. His faithfulness and kindness are more evident in our darker moments.

I don't want to waste the time by depending only on what I see now or what I expect to happen. Where would the faith be? I don't want to miss walking by faith in my Savior, the Giver of time and healing.

Isaiah shared the importance of faith: "If you do not stand firm in your faith, you will not stand at all" (7:9). It is hard to stand firm if we are walking by sight. It is only by faith that we can persevere as we heal, trusting and resting in our Lord and his perfect timing.

Scripture

> I wait for the LORD, my whole being waits,
>   and in his word I put my hope.
> I wait for the LORD
>   more than watchmen wait for the morning,
>   more than watchmen wait for the morning. (Ps 130:5–6)

Questions

1. What has taken more time than you thought it should?

2. How do you acknowledge pain and sadness but not dwell in it?

3. How has God brought healing in an area of your life?

Prayer

I thank you for healing. I thank you for times of waiting when I want to move on but can't. It is tempting to grow bitter, but my only good option is trusting in you. May I stand firm in my faith as I look to you, even with what I may be facing today. Amen.

43
Me and My Frother: A Life Lesson

A frother changed my life. OK, maybe that is a bit dramatic, but it really did change how much I enjoy my coffee. I used to drink coffee black (with lots of sugar). Then we moved to Spain, and I started drinking "cafe con leche" and cappuccinos. Frothy milk made coffee taste amazing. I loved going out for coffee more than ever.

Then, a friend gave me a frother of my very own. I could use it at home and make my own frothy coffee. Now if I want to, I can have warm, frothy milk in my coffee every day.

I love my frother (sorry for more drama—I like it a lot). It is amazing. I heat up the milk and add a little sugar. Then I turn on my battery-operated frother and froth away. I combine the frothy milk with coffee and get ready to experience liquid yumminess.

Recently, my milk hasn't been very foamy. I started frothing the milk a little longer and it was OK, but it wasn't like it used to be. The change happened so gradually that I didn't realize it. I began to forget what frothy milk tasted like. I haven't been to a restaurant in months, so I didn't have anything to which I could compare it.

But I wondered about it as it was taking longer and longer for my trusty frother to do its thing. And its thing was no longer what it once was.

I hadn't changed the milk I used. I had the same brand of coffee.

But it wasn't the same. I accepted my new reality, a little sad, but what can one do?

Don made coffee one morning. The milk was foamier than ever! I was so happy. What happened?

My hero realized my frother's batteries were low and put in new ones. My frother was dying, and I didn't even know it. It needed help. But it happened so slowly over time that I adapted to the new normal of whatever foaminess it could produce. It wasn't quite right, but it was what I had.

We can be like my frother. We may feel tired, stressed, and drained. But it happens over time, and we adjust to the new normal and forget what full energy feels like. So, we keep going, though a bit slower. We may think about diet, exercise, packed schedules, or what might be causing our fatigue. But there are so many ministry opportunities, we assume we can't or shouldn't stop. We keep going, but we are moving more and more slowly with less and less energy.

We don't take a day off.

We can't remember our last Sabbath rest.

We can't afford a vacation.

There are so many needs. Isn't stopping selfish? We don't realize we need recharged. Our batteries are dying. We need help. We must take the time to get recharged. We must be intentional; recharging doesn't happen without effort.

Take a weekly day of rest. Every week. Relax. Exercise. Have a fun day. Enjoy a hobby. Listen to your favorite music. Read a good book. Take a walk. Go to a movie. Watch children play in a park. Pet a dog. Sit in silence. Breathe.

Buy a frother!

Don't let your batteries die. Learn this life lesson from me and my recharged, fully functioning, happiness-inducing, delight-giving frother: Choose to recharge.

Scripture

> Remember the Sabbath day by keeping it holy. Six days you shall labor and do all your work, but the seventh day is a sabbath to the LORD your God. On it you shall not do any work, neither you, nor your son or daughter, nor your male or female servant, nor your animals, nor any foreigner residing in your towns For in six days the LORD made the heavens and the earth, the sea, and all that is in them, but he rested on the seventh day. Therefore the LORD blessed the Sabbath day and made it holy. (Exod 20:8–11)

Questions

1. When was your most recent day off?

2. How is your energy level usually? More drained or energized? Elaborate.

3. What stress symptoms are you experiencing?

Prayer

Thank you for times of rest. I recognize that I need breaks, I can't work nonstop. Help me recognize when I am too busy. Enable me to listen when others voice concern over my hectic schedule. May I serve wisely and well. (And thank you for my frother.) Amen.

44
Upended by COVID-19 but Not Undone

It seemed the world went mad. Some lived in fear; others faced anger. Some lived alone; some wished they lived alone! Homeschooling parents and those who never intended to homeschool worked hard to help their kids.

Some thought the coronavirus was a conspiracy. Others lost loved ones. We watched the numbers climbing. Medical equipment was lacking; hospitals were overrun. Some places were more devastated than others. Most public schools finished the year online.

We canceled three trips and were unsure about the next one. We could only go out of our apartment for necessities. My outside world was now my balcony with four slightly wilted potted plants.

It was crazy. Who could have imagined such a global upheaval?

I was reading about Joseph in Genesis and wondered if he thought the world had gone mad as well. Betrayed by his brothers and stripped of his special coat, he went from being a favored son to a common slave. As a teen, he went from being free to roam the countryside to a foreign place he could not escape.

The truth that made all the difference in the mayhem was this: The Lord was with Joseph. We see that phrase each time his life gets upended.

In his first place of service, Joseph prospered because God was with him (Gen 39:2). This was evident to Potiphar, his master, so he let Joseph run the house and take care of everything. Things were going well. Joseph was adapting. Until Potiphar's wife tried to seduce him. Joseph ran from temptation—doing the right thing. In revenge, Potiphar's wife cast blame on Joseph saying he tried to rape her. Joseph, disbelieved by the man who had once trusted him, was thrown into prison. For doing what was right.

Upended once more.

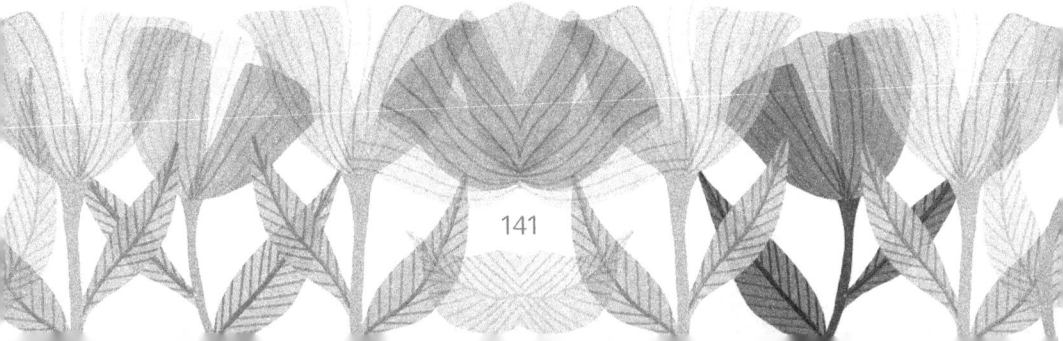

Memories of his brothers throwing him into the pit assailed him as he readjusted to life in a dank dungeon. Again, we see familiar words, "the LORD was with him; he showed him kindness and granted him favor in the eyes of the prison warden" (Gen 39:21). God was not only with him, he showed him kindness. Once again Joseph is adapting to unexpected circumstances that rocked his world.

After a while, Pharaoh's chief cup bearer and chief baker ended up in prison. Each had a dream that Joseph interpreted. One was killed and the other was freed as Joseph had predicted. Joseph asked the freed one to remember him and try to get him released from prison since he had done nothing wrong. Joseph had hope that he would be set free once the cupbearer mentioned him to Pharaoh.

The cupbearer forgot. Hope decreased daily in the following two years. Psalm 105:18–19 offers insight into Joseph's circumstances: "They bruised his feet with shackles, his neck was put in irons, till what he foretold came to pass, till the word of the LORD proved him true." Joseph, waiting on God's timing, seemed stuck.

Then Pharaoh had a dream and wanted to know what it meant. The cupbearer finally remembered Joseph.

Pharaoh sent for Joseph and told him his dream. Joseph knew he could not interpret it, but he also knew God was with him and could help him interpret the dream, which he did. Joseph, now thirty years of age, was put in command over Egypt, second only to Pharaoh. He led well and saved many lives due to wisely using the seven years of plenty to prepare for the seven years of famine.

Did Joseph know the Lord was with him or was this truth written in hindsight as the author looked over Joseph's life? Joseph knew it. He didn't despair. He didn't deny his suffering, but he didn't succumb to it either.

- He named his second son Ephraim, meaning God had made him fruitful in the land of his suffering.
- He forgave his brothers and saved their whole family (and many others) from starvation.
- He saw that God had sent him to Egypt, not his brothers. Though they intended Joseph harm, God intended good not only for him but for many nations.

When the world seemed crazy and Joseph's life turned upside down, the Lord was with him. Joseph experienced the Lord's presence as a young man. As an old man he could trace his life and see all God had done.

The Lord is with us. Our lives may have been upended, but we are not undone. We can know his presence now and live with hope. Years from now, we, too, will be able to look back and trace the hand of God. He will accomplish all his good purposes.

The psalmist reminds us in Psalm 23:4: "Even though I walk through the darkest valley, I will fear no evil, for you are with me."

Whether free to explore the world or unable to leave our homes, we are never undone and never alone. The Lord is with us.

Scripture

Then Joseph said to his brothers, "Come close to me." When they had done so, he said, "I am your brother Joseph, the one you sold into Egypt! And now, do not be distressed and do not be angry with yourselves for selling me here, because it was to save lives that God sent me ahead of you. For two years now there has been famine in the land, and for the next five years there will be no plowing and reaping. But God sent me ahead of you to preserve for you a remnant on earth and to save your lives by a great deliverance.

"So then, it was not you who sent me here, but God. He made me father to Pharaoh, lord of his entire household and ruler of all Egypt." (Gen 45:4–8)

Questions

1. What current situation leaves you feeling upended?

2. What experience of God's purposeful intervention in the past gives you hope?

3. How can you be an encouragement to others struggling in the present?

Prayer

Thank you that no matter what is happening around me, you see it and know all things. You know the problems, solutions, and what is your good purpose. I am not on my own even when the world has gone mad. There is so much evil, hatred, and rage in people's hearts. I fear for my nation and the lives of those who seek refuge here. May I remember you are with me. Give me power and courage to trust you and lead others to trust in you too. Amen.

45
Legacy: Earrings and Beyond

It's been almost one year since my mom left this temporary home to go to her eternal one. In the last few years of her life, she would talk about the jewelry she was leaving to me and my sister. She didn't want us to fight over it. My sister alleviated her concerns by telling her, "Mom, you have nice things but nothing worth losing relationships over."

It is true. My sister is almost always right! As we enjoy some of the tangibles mom left us, we realize her biggest legacy is not what we hold in our hands. She left us so much more! Her lasting legacy includes love for family, faithfulness, and loyalty. With that legacy, there wasn't a lust for more things, but a longing to love and comfort one another.

Mom was also a woman of faith. She knew Jesus and trusted her heavenly Father. On one of her visits to the hospital she said she wasn't afraid. She knew God was with her. And now, though I miss her, I know she is with God. Forever.

One of the things I have from my mom is a pair of earrings she wore. I like wearing them. Though I need no reminder to think of her, whenever I put them on, I remember her and realize anew how much I miss her. They are not priceless in the world's economy, but they belonged to my mom and are special to me.

When we were visiting family earlier this year, I put them on in the morning and went out to meet friends for lunch. At one point, I passed a mirror and noticed one of them was missing. My heart fell. Where could it be? How did I lose it? I retraced steps. I searched all around where I sat in the car. Nowhere. Trying to be present as I chatted with friends, I had to focus my mind on the here and now and not where I might have lost the earring earlier in the day. When we arrived back at our son's home where we were staying, I retraced more steps and went into the bedroom where I had put them on. The earring had fallen on the floor. I found it!

I'm wearing them again as I write. In the future, I may lose one of them again or maybe both! They may break. When I leave this world, I won't take them with me. (In heaven—where by God's grace I'm going—the streets are paved with gold and jewels already there outshine the brightest gems on earth.) None of us take anything with us on that final journey. Maybe my children and grandchildren will be fond of some of my trinkets … but this kind of inheritance will always stay on earth. I'm happy they can enjoy the physical things we may be able to leave them. I hope that they think of me with as much love as I feel when I think of my mom. I also long to leave them more than a temporary inheritance.

The legacy I would love to leave my family is the preciousness of faith in Jesus. It is only through him we can have an everlasting inheritance. A legacy of grace will never end. As my mom is relishing time with her Savior, she would wholeheartedly agree. Mom was generous. She would be tickled that I find delight in wearing her earrings now. Mom was also wise. She knew that a lasting legacy is not what we clasp in our hands but what is held in our souls.

Scripture

Praise be to the God and Father of our Lord Jesus Christ! In his great mercy he has given us new birth into a living hope through the resurrection of Jesus Christ from the dead, and into an inheritance that can never perish, spoil or fade. This inheritance is kept in heaven for you, who through faith are shielded by God's power until the coming of the salvation that is ready to be revealed in the last time. In all this you greatly rejoice, though now for a little while you may have had to suffer grief in all kinds of trials. These have come so that the proven genuineness of your faith—of greater worth than gold, which perishes even though refined by fire—may result in praise, glory and honor when Jesus Christ is revealed. (1 Pet 1:3–7)

Questions

1. What kind of legacy would you like to leave?

2. What needs to happen in order to leave the legacy you want?

3. How would you paraphrase 1 Peter 1:3–7?

Prayer

Thank you for the legacy my loved ones have left me. My mom, my in-laws, pastors, and co-workers. I have been blessed by all that I learned from them and their walks of faith. I ask that I would live a life of faith that would be a blessing for those coming after me. Please empower me to serve you and leave a lasting legacy for your glory. Amen.

46
Anxiety About Tomorrow Imprisons Me Today

When COVID-19 hit, there was a lot of anxiety. Most anxiety is based on what will, might, or could happen in the future. We didn't know how fast the virus would keep spreading. We didn't know if loved ones might become infected and how they would react to it. We didn't know whether to travel or how often to go out in public.

The COVID-19 virus affected older people more seriously. When I researched to discover what is meant by older, I learned that it is being over sixty.

OK. That includes me—I am officially "older" in Google's opinion.

When something happens outside of our control, fear is the most normal response. A public widespread illness or a dreaded personal diagnosis makes us more aware of our limitations. There are some things we are powerless to stop. We can take steps. We can be wise. We can be proactive. But we may not be successful.

The truth is we are never really in control. We face certain situations that make us more aware of this. We lack the ability to make things behave the way we want.

Paul tells us not to be anxious about anything. He writes in Philippians 4:6–7:

> Do not be anxious about anything, but in every situation, by prayer and petition, with thanksgiving, present your requests to God. And the peace of God, which transcends all understanding, will guard your hearts and your minds in Christ Jesus.

But he also mentions his own anxiety earlier in his letter. Paul states in Philippians 2:28, "Therefore I am all the more eager to send him, so that when you see him again you may be glad and I may have less anxiety."

Anxiety, fear, and nervousness are all natural responses to big, scary things. The problem comes when anxiety controls us because we think our puny strength is our only resource. We act as if we should be able to conquer the impossible, and we can't. We forget that God is the only all-able one. Paul knew what anxiety was. He felt it. He also knew how to handle it. He turned to the Lord.

One word helps me when I am feeling anxious. Today. God has given me today. He has not promised me tomorrow. Whenever I am praying and unloading my burdens to God, they are almost always future-based. And it is good to give him those concerns. Tomorrows are God's domain, not mine.

I have today. With the gift of life he gives today, I can serve him. With the breath that he gives today, I can bless his name. I can proclaim to others his faithfulness as current events reveal limits to what we can control. With his strength this day, you and I can walk by faith. We can entrust to him worldwide viruses, conflicts, and changes … along with all the other unknowns that tomorrow may bring.

Anxiety takes us captive when we take future possibilities on today.

I may feel anxious about what may happen tomorrow. But today I am healthy. I don't have to surrender to anxiety. I can pray to the all-able One. I can present my requests to God and expect his promised peace to fill my heart and set me free.

There are those for whom anxiety is a deeper issue than trusting God today for tomorrows. May God guide you to find good help as you walk by faith when the way seems dark.

Scripture

> Who of you by worrying can add a single hour to your life? Since you cannot do this very little thing, why do you worry about the rest?

> Consider how the wild flowers grow. They do not labor or spin. Yet I tell you, not even Solomon in all his splendor was dressed like one of these. If that is how God clothes the grass of the field, which is here today, and tomorrow is thrown into the fire, how much more will he clothe you—you of little faith! (Luke 12:25–28)

Questions

1. What is an area that is easy for you to worry about?

2. How do you know when someone needs professional help with anxiety?

3. What are your plans today? How can you leave tomorrow in God's hands?

Prayer

Thank you for today. It made me feel a bit better to read that Paul knew some anxiety, but I am grateful he learned how to handle it. May I be wise as I trust you today and leave tomorrow in your hands. I choose not to be a prisoner of worry and what ifs. You have set me free. Amen.

47
Adjusting to a "To-Go Cup" Mindset

I moved back to my home country, but I knew that transitioning after living overseas wouldn't be easy. I bought a book about reentry to work through. I got a journal to write in so that I could reflect on what I read. I chose a morning to walk to a nearby coffee shop—book, pen, and journal in hand. I was expectant, ready to learn what I needed to learn to return well.

I decided to order what I missed when living overseas. I asked for an asiago cheese bagel, my favorite. I ordered a latte thinking it was the closest thing to a "café con leche" in Spain. And I could order in English. This was going to be good.

Until she said, "We are all out of asiago cheese bagels."

Well, these things happen. Only slightly miffed, I could still spend my morning learning to return well.

They called my name to get my coffee.

It was in a to-go cup. Why would they give a to-go cup to a to-stay person? It didn't come with sugar, so I walked over to get some. I took the lid off to put the sugar in and saw the airy foam on top. Not my normal frothy milk. I stirred in the sugar as best I could with a wooden stick, took a sip and added a bit more sugar. I finally got it to taste mediocre.

But the coffee *wasn't* café con leche. It wasn't in a mug. I felt disenchanted. Disappointed—but also determined to return well. I began reading chapter 1.

I couldn't concentrate. My expectations of coffee, surroundings, and a mug were all based on what I had come to know and love in Spain. I wasn't there. I was here and there was no asiago cheese bagel to take away the sting. I felt like standing up and saying to the coffee shop, "I am trying to return well but you are not helping!"

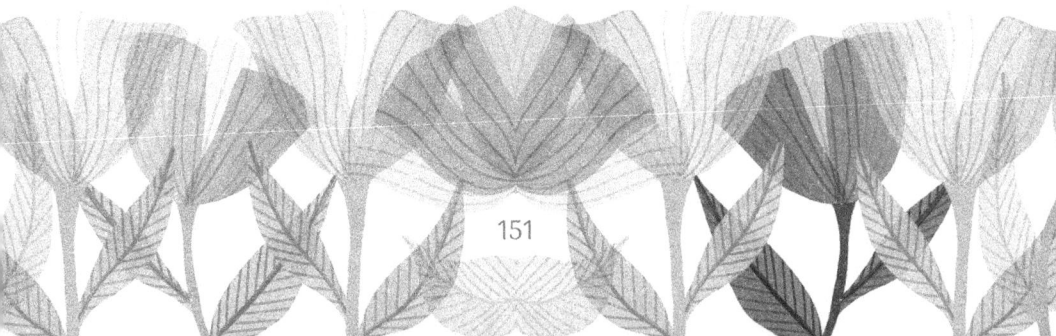

I'm so thankful that in my 60-plus years of living I have learned how to control my temper tantrums. I continued to drink my coffee. I read the first few chapters of the book and thought a bit about what I read. But I didn't write anything down. My journal was blank.

I haven't been back to the coffee shop. I haven't opened the book since then. I still want to return well, but maybe I need more time or a different setting to learn how to do that.

Before moving forward, I need to reexamine my expectations. I didn't realize the images in my head of this coffee and reflection time were tied to Spain, not here. I had become comfortable there, knew what to expect, and enjoyed a lot of it. My anticipation of the coffee shop was based on where I used to live and not where I am. I didn't realize my expectations were unrealistic until they weren't met.

I also need to look at timing. We hadn't been back very long when I first tried to process our transition and we are still very much in limbo. It might have been too soon. So, I am going to try to learn about returning well after I feel more settled. I didn't have the emotional capacity to process how to return well because I didn't feel like I'd truly returned.

Whatever steps I take in my journey to return well, I need to think through expectations. With the passing of each day, I will feel more like I have returned. Disillusioned with my first try, I am more determined to learn about returning well. I realize I must try new approaches until I discover what works best for me.

I am discovering that returning well is a process, not an event. May I be intentional and have an open heart in this transition. I look forward to diving into the topic again and journaling about returning well.

And one day I will be able to say, I returned well—even if I must add the word "eventually."

Scripture

LORD, you alone are my portion and my cup;
  you make my lot secure.
The boundary lines have fallen for me in pleasant places;
  surely I have a delightful inheritance.
I will praise the LORD, who counsels me;
  even at night my heart instructs me.
I keep my eyes always on the LORD.
  With him at my right hand, I will not be shaken.

(Ps 16:5–8)

Questions

1. How have you found transitions challenging?

2. What helps you to transition well?

3. How do expectations play a role in the frustrations of transitions?

Prayer

You never change. We are always facing change. You are a rock, our anchor—through change you hold us so that we are not shaken. Thank you for your strong grip. I am grateful for your steadying hand in the middle of all the changes I face. Amen.

48
God Is Near and There

I remember sitting in theology class and hearing the term "omnipresent." God is not bound by space or time. He is here. He is there. He is everywhere at the same time. This concept boggled my mind. It was a big thought for a tiny brain. I thought it was cool and amazing, but I would have never thought of it as comforting.

Until I moved overseas and began serving in cross-cultural ministry. I moved away from family and missed special family events. I found myself far from the known and flung into the uncomfortable. Who knew I could feel so lonely when surrounded by people? I knew that God was with me here. I recognized, too, that God was also with my family there. For the first time, his omnipresence was consoling to me.

When my grandpa was dying and I couldn't be there, God was near him. But he was also with me, comforting me as I grieved six thousand miles away.

When my husband still wasn't home in the wee hours of the morning, I panicked. He was driving on a road nicknamed by locals "way of death" in a car brand known as "flying coffins." I knew he was with me. But I forgot God was also with him. The Lord saw my anxiety as I tried to find out where Don was. God knew. Through various phone calls, I discovered Don's rescheduled departure time. I had pictured him hurt and lying on the side of the road. I needed to remember that God was with both of us no matter what.

When some of my grandbabies were born and I couldn't get there in time for their arrival, God was already there. And he was with me in my excitement at their birth and stark disappointment at not being there.

Weeping as I got texts about how my mom was doing in her last hours before entering her heavenly home, God was with me. He was also with my dad, sister, and other family members as they were with her to say goodbye. He was also with my mom as he welcomed her home.

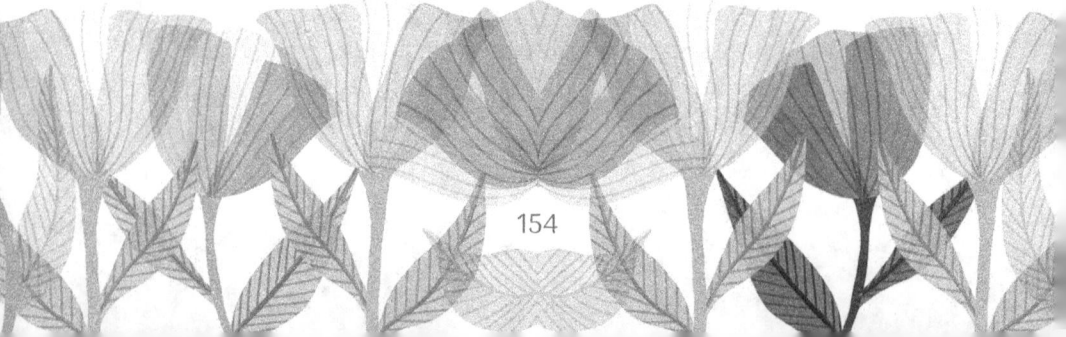

Hearing news about people we love when we aren't there is difficult. Even when I know there is nothing I can do to help by being there, it is still hard. I want to be present, near those I love, especially when they are hurting. When consumed with an overwhelming desire to be there, I go back to this truth and feel reassured. God is near me. God is near them. He is everywhere all the time. Never has this truth been more special than when I recognize and accept that I can only be here. I can't be there with every loved one, every pain, every sorrow. But he can.

And so, I can turn to the God of all comfort where I am. Loved ones can turn to the Father of compassion where they are. He is never too busy, never too far, but always near us wherever we are. We discover that in every place the Lord is our comforter.

I am grateful that God is who he is. Knowing he is never surprised, never at a loss, never far away, but always near, gives my soul hope. Regardless of where we are, he is near and offers peace and comfort to all who look to him.

Scripture

Praise be to the God and Father of our Lord Jesus Christ, the Father of compassion and the God of all comfort, who comforts us in all our troubles, so that we can comfort those in any trouble with the comfort we ourselves receive from God. (2 Cor 1:3–4)

Questions

1. How is the omnipresence of God a comfort for you?

2. What do you need to grieve well?

3. How has someone comforted you in a meaningful way?

Prayer

You are near and far. You are the God of all comfort. You enfold me into your everlasting arms, you uphold me and fill my heart with peace. You see my grief and don't turn away. You aren't embarrassed by my tears, frizzy hair, and swollen red eyes. I receive comfort from you and am blessed. Amen.

49

What About Blob?

I had fallen asleep in the car, my head tilted in an unnatural angle and my mouth probably slightly ajar. Hopefully, there was no drool; however, since I was sleeping, I will never know! As I awoke, I stretched and rubbed my neck. For the first time I noticed a lump on the right side of my neck. How unusual. I assumed I had pulled a muscle or something. But it didn't go away. I went to the doctor who ordered blood tests, cat scans, ultrasounds, and an MRI to try to determine what it was. It was not a pulled muscle.

The testing determined the lump to be a four-centimeter sized tumor stemming from my spine. I dislike the word "tumor" as it has so many negative connotations in my mind. My daughter and I explored synonyms to come up with a word less traumatic for me. We found many that were even worse than tumor! However, one of the synonyms that got us giggling was "blob" because we were reminded of the movie, "What about Bob?" Thus, we started calling the tumor Blob and asking, "What about Blob?" We thought and prayed about what treatment to choose. There were no easy answers. Surgery might be a risk since Blob was so close to the nerve that affected my right arm. I didn't like having Blob invade my space.

In life, though, sometimes we encounter unexpected, uninvited, and unwanted things. My initial response is usually fear as I realize I have so little control over so much that I encounter. I left the hospital consultation, trying to figure out what this uninvited guest might mean to my life, my future, and my own desires. After recognizing my limited knowledge of the future and what it might look like, I took the time to look to God and ponder what his purposes might be. How could he use this in my life for his glory? After all, Blob was only unexpected to me. I was surprised, but God knew all along, eons before I was even born, that this uninvited guest would be allowed to enter my body. God holds tomorrow in his hands.

He has my life securely and unshakably in his hands and he has plans to use all things, even Blob, for his glory and my good. I find great hope, joy, and comfort in that.

I began to reflect on my own mortality, the sweetness of life and the many blessings I have enjoyed. It was quite amazing to realize that I have few regrets in life, not much left unsaid to those I love, and no doubts when I go home with Jesus that God's faithfulness remains certain to future generations.

I reread Acts 13:36a about David's time on earth. Luke wrote, "Now when David had served God's purpose in his own generation, he fell asleep." It wasn't until David had accomplished what God had purposed for him that David entered his heavenly home. It reminded me that my life is in God's hands, and I know that I will be here long enough to accomplish the purposes God has for me. The psalmist reminds us in Psalm 138:8a (ESV), "The LORD will fulfill his purposes for me." I don't know all his purposes for me or how long it will take to fulfill them. No one does. Blob's invasion doesn't mean my life is over. Even without Blob, it doesn't mean I would live another day. What I do know is that, by God's grace and strength, I will have the time needed to fulfill the purposes God has for me.

As I talked with doctors and made decisions about Blob, I did so knowing that God is sovereign and good. He has known from eternity past about my uninvited guest, and he has no doubts about what is best for me when I ask him, "What about Blob?"

Scripture

> But the Lord is faithful, and he will strengthen you and protect you from the evil one. We have confidence in the Lord that you are doing and will continue to do the things we command. May the Lord direct your hearts into God's love and Christ's perseverance. (2 Thess 3:3–5)

Questions

1. What has been unexpected in your life recently?

2. What is your initial reaction to events that you don't feel prepared for?

3. How would you state God's purpose for you as you understand it today?

Prayer

I am so grateful you know what is ahead of me. You are always prepared, never surprised, always eternally sovereign over everything. You are aware of little surprises and big shocks. You know what my reaction will be to what is next and how you will use it in my life. Thank you for what I've been learning through Blob about me and you. Amen.

50
Lessons from Blob

I am so deeply grateful for the prayers of God's people when I had surgery to get rid of the tumor I call "Blob." After much testing and consultation, the neurosurgeon determined that the surgery wasn't as close to the artery as it could have been. I don't think three millimeters is all that far, but I guess in this kind of surgery it is a safe distance!

After five days in the hospital, I went home, grasping my pain medicine tightly. The main problems were shoulder pain, numbness, shooting pains, and tingling sensations. Since they had to leave a little bit of Blob inside to keep arm movement as normal as possible, we will be monitoring him. But first, I needed to recover from surgery.

When I got my stitches out, before I saw the scar, I asked Don on a scale of 1–10, with one looking more like Cinderella and ten looking more like Frankenstein, what did my neck look like? He smiled and teasingly called me "Frank"! Really, though, the scar isn't so bad. I have decided to see it as a reminder of God's goodness and his provision for me.

One lesson I am continuing to learn as I deal with Blob is that fear and worry are always ready to pounce. As I read over the medical report, I saw that during surgery there was brisk bleeding. How brisk is brisk, and how do I know it won't just start again? Could I bleed to death? What if my arm hurts like this for the rest of my life? Was having surgery a mistake? What if Blob grows and overtakes my body until there is nothing left of me? There were serious concerns that give me pause and plain idiotic notions that still caused alarm though I knew in my head they were crazy.

In response to some legitimate concerns as well as foolish, unfounded fears I come back to knowing that I am never alone. I wasn't alone in the operating room when I was briskly bleeding. I wasn't alone in the ICU when my heart rate spiked. I wasn't alone when I woke up in my cubicle and no one else was visible. God was there with me, totally calm and very aware of what was happening with me.

I am not alone. He is Lord of the present. He is the God of the future so I will not be alone tomorrow. Even if my arm never heals or even if my most wild imaginations come to pass and Blob not only overtakes me but the world, God would not be taken by surprise. He would know exactly what to do to take care of Blob and bring glory to the name of Jesus.

I choose not to dwell on what Blob has done in the past or worry about what Blob might do in the future. My choice is to live today, by God's grace, with full assurance of his presence and help. Blob isn't under my control—as a matter of fact, very little is. Blob is under the Lord's authority and the Lord always knows the best thing to do and does it—everyday.

Scripture

Then Moses summoned Joshua and said to him in the presence of all Israel, "Be strong and courageous, for you must go with this people into the land that the LORD swore to their ancestors to give them, and you must divide it among them as their inheritance. The LORD himself goes before you and will be with you; he will never leave you nor forsake you. Do not be afraid; do not be discouraged." (Deut 31:7–8)

Questions

1. How have you seen God's hand in the past?

2. What is God doing in your life today?

3. What are some fears you can surrender to him as you face tomorrow?

Prayer

You are Lord of Lords. You are not bound by space or time. There is nothing too hard for you. You are our sovereign king. May I boldly follow you and trust you as I enter the unknown. Amen.

51
The Panic Button

I needed an MRI to see what Blob was up to. I arrived at the hospital. This was not my first MRI, so I knew what to expect. I changed into the familiar green outfit and lay down on the table that would slide into the tunnel. The technician was explaining to me not to move, not to swallow when I heard the machine making noises, and to keep my eyes shut. He then put the panic button into my hands so that if I needed anything I could push it. I didn't think I would need it, after all I had done this before, and it wasn't too bad. But it was comforting to know I had it just in case.

I lay still, strapped onto the table as it slid into the MRI tunnel. The pings and whirrs of the machine began. I knew I shouldn't swallow. He said not to. However, the more I thought about being told not to swallow the more I had to swallow. I told myself I didn't need to swallow. I wasn't convincing enough and I swallowed. And then I had to swallow again. One, two or three swallows later I renewed my efforts to stop!

To pass the time I tried to come up with songs in my head to match the beats of the machine noises. I found a few oldies that almost worked. Alas, the machine was not cooperating and after a few lines, it didn't follow my lead as it kept changing tempos.

I grew tired singing songs in my head that didn't harmonize with the machine. I prayed, I went over some Scripture verses, and in between those times I was thinking it was taking a long time. Finally, the machine was quiet and expectantly I waited for someone to come get me out of the tunnel.

No one came. I waited and waited some more.

I told myself to count to one hundred and if no one came by the end I could push my panic button. No worries. Be calm. I even counted slowly. As I neared one hundred it seemed as if the silence was deafening. Where was everyone? I didn't want to be in the tunnel anymore. I decided to push the panic button.

Now I know why they call it a panic button. When you push it and nothing happens, you start to panic. I pushed it again … and again … and again. Silence. No one was coming. Was it broken? Were they ignoring me? Did they leave and if so, why?

I tried calling out. "Hello. Is anyone there?" Silence reigned except for the slight echo of my own voice inside of the tunnel.

I kept squeezing the panic button as I considered my options. Maybe I was pushing it wrong. I pushed at it from all different angles. Nothing changed. In between telling myself not to worry and yet feeling my heart rate increase, I prayed again for help and began to plan how I could break out of the tunnel.

On the narrow table I tried jiggling my arms and wiggling my legs. I looked around to figure out if I could squirm enough to slide down the table and out of the tunnel. It didn't look promising.

I prayed some more. I knew God was with me—and he was the only one as far as I could tell from my current tunnel vision! He is always there, and he does bring a sense of calmness. But I couldn't see him and I really wanted out!

As I was becoming desperate enough to try and scoot down the table to make an escape, I heard someone coming. I felt the table sliding and was so very relieved to know that I was getting out. The technician mentioned a complication about inserting the dye for the contrasting MRI and said we had to postpone it until next week. That I was coming back again the following week didn't really sink in as I was too busy savoring my freedom. Then it hit.

Wait. Next week I am scheduled to be in the tunnel again. Oh, wow. That was a disheartening thought. However, until then I can swallow as much as I want and I am free to roam, sing, and relish moving around without restraint. I have time to think of more songs and I can have my prayer list ready.

And maybe I can ask them to replace the panic button with a calm button! Or even better, I can realize anew that even though I can't see God, he promises never to leave me. It only *looks* like I am alone. He was in the tunnel with me and next week when I find myself in the bowels of the MRI machine again, I know I'm not the only one in there. It will be God and me together. Just like always.

Now that is more calming than any button!

P.S. The next week, when the MRI technician gave me the panic button, I asked him if it worked. He said, "Of course," and pushed it. Nothing happened. He left the room and when he returned said, "It is working now."

Scripture

A time is coming and in fact has come when you will be scattered, each to your own home. You will leave me all alone. Yet I am not alone, for my Father is with me.

(John 16:32)

Questions

1. When was your most recent opportunity to panic?

2. What happens when you feel forgotten?

3. What difference does it make knowing God is with you when you face hardship?

Prayer

I can't see you so sometimes I forget you are with me. I am tempted to think I must handle everything on my own. Forgive me for neglecting your perfect presence. I am grateful you are with me in tight places. Though no one else is there, you are. Amen.

52
From Selfies to Otheries!

I remember learning what a selfie is. I am not sure who took the first one. I know that they are popular and are frequently seen on social media. I didn't know selfie was a real word until I found it in an online dictionary. It basically said that it is when a picture of me is taken by me so that I can post it on social media.

There is a part of us that wants to share our lives with others. We post pictures of ourselves, our families, food we eat, and places that we visit. We want to connect with others. There may be some instances where taking selfies represents a me-centric worldview where it is all too easy to focus on myself … my comfort, my pleasure, my appearance. I read a selfie tip that to help yourself look slimmer or appear to have bigger eyes you take a picture by holding the camera up at a higher angle. When I try to take a selfie, it doesn't seem to matter what angle I hold the camera, often part of me is missing. So, I guess that would make me look slimmer!

We don't read in the New Testament about selfies. However, there is a definite emphasis on one another! The Scriptures teach that we honor one another above ourselves, that we look out for the interests of others, not just our own. We are to love, forgive, and bear with one another. We are to be devoted to one another. The Bible doesn't really teach us to focus on ourselves.

Maybe as believers we can start taking "otheries." How can I promote another person's welfare above my own? How can I honor my teammate? In what ways can I show esteem to my leader? Am I as devoted as I should be to others? What can I do to serve my friends?

One area of confusion for me is figuring out when I am practicing good self-care by setting healthy boundaries and when am I being selfish. My tendency is to be selfish anyway, to consider my own needs above another person's. I also know that the Bible teaches me to be generous and value others more than myself (Phil 2:3). Yet, if we never say no or take time for ourselves, we will probably burn out and become unable to serve anyone until we heal.

When I need to discern my priorities and choices, I think about Jesus and how he lived and served. We read in each of the gospels that at times he would go away by himself to pray. But there is also story after story of how consistently he loved, spent time with, and served others. He set aside time for himself and his walk with God and that strengthened him for his ministry to others. We learn that it is possible to take care of ourselves without becoming stuck in selfishness. May our love for God and for others guide us as we serve.

By God's grace and power may we grow less "selfie" and more "otherie" in our love for one another!

Scripture

Be completely humble and gentle; be patient, bearing with one another in love. Make every effort to keep the unity of the Spirit through the bond of peace. (Eph 4:2–3)

Questions

1. How do you see selfishness in your corner of the world?

2. How can we love one another well?

3. How can we use social media for the good of others?

Prayer

You have commanded us to love one another. It is sad to see how quickly I can become self-focused. May I be sensitive to your leading and proactive in loving my brothers and sisters. When I get off kilter, convict me and enable me to respond quickly. Amen.

53
Optimism or Pessimism

About to witness a spectacularly romantic sunset on a California beach, Don and I were walking slowly with our arms around each other. Don was saying something about this being our last night in California and what a beautiful evening it was. I was listening to him, but at the same time I noticed a seagull flying overhead. It was about to fly directly over our heads, and I said, "I sure hope that bird doesn't poop on my head!"

The romantic moment quickly dissipated. Rather than focusing on the beauty all around me and the person with whom I was walking, my attention was snared by the possibility of a negative event that might not even happen! In my defense, birds have pooped on my head four times on three different continents (once indoors!). It was not a pleasant experience.

In life, how can we live in and enjoy the present and not give into worry about what might happen? What is the difference between optimism and pessimism? How does Jesus call us to live?

After sharing with his disciples about their upcoming struggles and his own departure Jesus said, "I have told you these things, so that in me you may have peace. In this world you will have trouble. But take heart! I have overcome the world" (John 16:33).

Jesus knows that there is trouble in this world, but he also knows that he has overcome it. We recognize evil, but we are not overcome by it to the point of despair. Rather, we are to have peace and to take heart. Jesus is never worried about what might happen.

Optimism and pessimism are attitudes focused on future possibilities. Pessimism looks at the future and thinks bad things might happen. Optimism looks at the future and expects good things. As believers, we know that good or bad can happen, but our trust is in God who rules over all things and fulfills his purposes through all that happens.

If I were looking at the beach scenario as a pessimist (which I tend to be), I would assume if poop was going to fly it was going to land on my head. If I were looking at it as an optimist (as Don is), I would have been enjoying the walk and my spouse, and the beauty of the bird in flight. If I were looking at the scenario as a humorist, I would think it funny if the bird pooped on the optimist's head. Then the pessimist could optimistically say, "I knew it was going to happen! I'm just glad it didn't happen to me!"

Whether you tend to be an optimist or a pessimist, remember that Jesus is sovereign over all, and we can trust him through all circumstances.

Scripture

When you go to war against your enemies and see horses and chariots and an army greater than yours, do not be afraid of them, because the LORD your God, who brought you up out of Egypt, will be with you. When you are about to go into battle, the priest shall come forward and address the army. He shall say: "Hear, Israel: Today you are going into battle against your enemies. Do not be fainthearted or afraid; do not panic or be terrified by them. For the LORD your God is the one who goes with you to fight for you against your enemies to give you victory." (Deut 20:1–4)

Questions

1. Would you describe yourself as an optimist or pessimist and why?

2. How does knowing Jesus rules over everything encourage you today?

3. If we want to walk by faith, how do we do this if we tend to be pessimistic?

Prayer

You are the sovereign one who goes with me. I don't need to be fainthearted or panic, even if I assume the worst is going to happen. I can trust you to use even the hard things for my good. As your follower, may faith fill my every step as I seek to do your will. Guard my heart from fear. Give needed grace today. Amen.

54
Fishing in Community

When I went fishing with my dad when I was younger, we each had our poles. We would put the bait on the hook, cast it into the water and wait. And wait. And sometimes wait some more.

I remember my dad helping me when I cast my line, but the hook got stuck in a nearby tree behind me. He patiently got the hook free and helped me cast the line where it needed to go. He gave me tips on when and where fish might be biting. His choice for bait when fishing with his daughters for blue gills was maggots. He taught my sister and me to bait our own hooks. When we needed help, he gave it. He could have had a more peaceful day of fishing with a lot less trouble without us tagging along, but he spent time with us and taught us how to fish.

I had read about the fishermen Jesus called to follow him to fish for men. I knew in my head that back then they used nets. However, because of what I have experienced and known about fishing, I always thought about fishing as an individual sport and therefore by association, thought the same about fishing for souls. We each go fishing; one by one we go fishing to catch one fish at a time. We can help each other, give tips, and encourage each other, but we are still each holding our own poles. When we catch a fish, we each bring in our catch and then we put the caught fish together in the bucket of water to keep them fresh until we finish fishing.

While on vacation at the beach in India, I woke up in the morning and ate breakfast outside across the street from the beach. It was beautiful. I watched fishermen each morning doing their jobs to catch fish. They would bring in the nets, prepare to cast them and together bring them in. There were also those who sat in the sun to repair the nets which were torn. I saw that fishing wasn't a one-at-a-time activity. It took a community to go fishing! There were those in the boat, others with the nets in the water, and still others pulling on the ropes from the shore helping to bring the nets in. The huge nets had many fish in them as the fishermen worked toward the same purpose alongside each other.

When Jesus called us to fish for people, he wasn't calling individuals to do the fishing independently from one another—he was calling communities of faith. He made us members of his body so that we serve him as one body though we are many members. We all must work together to go fishing, and it takes all of us to get the job done!

Scripture

> As Jesus was walking beside the Sea of Galilee, he saw two brothers, Simon called Peter and his brother Andrew. They were casting a net into the lake, for they were fishermen. "Come, follow me," Jesus said, "and I will send you out to fish for people." At once they left their nets and followed him. (Matt 4:18–20)

Questions

1. How can we be fishers of people as a community?

2. What are some challenges of fishing together with others?

3. How have you seen effectiveness as an individual sharing Christ with others?

Prayer

Thank you that I am not alone. I am a part of your body, a member of your family, and we serve you together. I have felt such pressure to be a fisher of people by myself, and I can share my faith and plant seeds. But to know that believers can work together to cast our nets wide and gather in those who believe is encouraging. Use me. Use us. Amen.

55
She Kept Pouring

A widow was about to lose her sons to pay off her dead husband's debts and she asked Elisha for help. Elisha asks her, "How can I help you? Tell me, what do you have in your house?" "Your servant has nothing there at all," she said, "except a small jar of olive oil" (2 Kgs 4:2–3).

You know the rest of the story. Elisha tells her to get jars, a lot of jars, and then fill them with the oil that she had. Her sons go around the neighborhood collecting empty jars and one by one she fills all the jars with her "little oil." I love the phrase "she kept pouring." She looked for more jars to fill until they ran out of jars—not oil!

At first, she discounted what little she had in light of how huge her need loomed before her. When she compared her little oil to the creditors coming to enslave her sons and having no husband to help her fight them, she couldn't see what a little bit of oil could do. Yet, in obedience when she used the little she had, by God's power, her little became a lot. She was not only able to pay off her creditors, but she also met the immediate needs of herself and her two sons, with a surplus for the future.

I love that story because often I think that I have nothing to offer except something little and that little seems trivial when the need in missions is so great. If someone were to figuratively ask me, "What do you have in your house?" I would be tempted to say that considering the great task he has called us to, "Your servant has nothing at all!" I forget about the little I have, and I forget about how big God is. I fail to remember the widow's oil and how she kept on pouring until her job was done!

In comparing what I have to offer with what I see others doing, it is tempting to think that what I have is so little it isn't worth contributing. I sometimes have doubts about my role—is it helping? Is what I do valuable? Is my small contribution effective?

I see others around the world doing bigger things, facing harsher circumstances, persevering through challenges and persecution for the glory of God.

Then there is me ... and my *little*.

My focus should not be on what little I have, nor the contribution of others, but on God who specializes in taking what is little and producing big. Remember the five loaves and two fish, the water at a wedding that became wine, a boy shepherd defeating a giant soldier? My response is to offer to the Lord willingly and gladly all that I am, as little as it may seem. God is powerful and able to use my little for his bigger purposes. It is his delight and pleasure to shine through cracked pots, to show his strength in our weakness, and to multiply all our littles for his big glory! I want to keep pouring until my job is done.

What do you have in your house?

Scripture

> Meanwhile, the Philistine, with his shield bearer in front of him, kept coming closer to David. He looked David over and saw that he was little more than a boy, glowing with health and handsome, and he despised him. He said to David, "Am I a dog, that you come at me with sticks?" And the Philistine cursed David by his gods. "Come here," he said, "and I'll give your flesh to the birds and the wild animals!"
>
> David said to the Philistine, "You come against me with sword and spear and javelin, but I come against you in the name of the LORD Almighty, the God of the armies of Israel, whom you have defied. This day the LORD will deliver you into my hands, and I'll strike you down and cut off your head. This very day I will give the carcasses of the Philistine army to the birds and the wild animals, and the whole world will know that there is a God in Israel."
>
> (1 Sam 17:41–46)

Questions

1. What little do you have to offer in contrast to the big that you want to see happen?

2. How do you "keep pouring" in your current circumstances?

3. How does David's battle with Goliath inspire you?

Prayer

Thank you for David's example of faith to you. His heart was committed to you and his life followed as he honored you through his service. You are a big God. It is true that I have little to offer, but you can use all I do have and bring glory to your name through it. May I be faithful to keep pouring out what I have by faith. Amen.

56
Evelyn's Legacy of Praying

When he heard that his grandma had gone to heaven one of my sons said to the other, "I'm a bit more nervous leaving the house now because grandma isn't here praying!" If there is one thing Grandma Lange was known for it is prayer.

Don's mom prayed daily for each of her children, grandchildren, and great grandchildren. She prayed for the lost, for her church, for people she had known a long time, and people she just met. She prayed for her community. She prayed for cross-cultural workers. She prayed for the world. She prayed. She prayed a lot.

At our family reunion a few years ago, she shared that she wished she had more money and resources to pass on to the family. She wasn't wealthy in the world's eyes. She was generous, though, and wanted to help more than she could. I remember looking around at the family as she shared what she wished she was able to give. We all knew she was forgetting what she actually gave, and many of us told her so. An inheritance isn't merely worldly things or earthly possessions. We received an invaluable inheritance from her.

She gave us a legacy of faith in God.

When her first husband died at the age of forty-six, she was a widow with four of the five children still at home. She prayed. God provided. When her oldest son offered to come back home and help, she declined. "God has called you to seminary." She prayed, knowing that God would take care of him and her. When her third son's lungs collapsed, she prayed. God rescued. When one of her daughters-in-law was in a traumatic car accident and not expected to live, she prayed. God intervened. When finances were tight, she prayed. God supplied. When her children needed shoes and food was scarce, she prayed. God answered. There was never a situation in life that left her defeated. She always had God.

When she needed surgery after a heart attack, she said, "This is a win-win situation. If I die, I go to see my Savior and the loved ones who have gone before me. If I live, I get to stay with my family and enjoy them until he calls me home." She continued to live and pray. As a matter of fact, she was on her way to a prayer meeting when she became very ill, and God called her home that evening.

We miss her, but this gift she has left us endures. Whenever any of us face a challenge, we pray. Whenever we are afraid, we pray. Whenever something looks impossible, we pray.

This is one of her lasting gifts to us. We know how to pray. She not only taught us this, but she also modeled a faith that saw God as always bigger, always stronger, always there. Nothing is too difficult for him. Knowing God, we pray.

We will miss this woman of faith but are thankful that her legacy continues.

Scripture

Epaphras, who is one of you and a servant of Christ Jesus, sends greetings. He is always wrestling in prayer for you, that you may stand firm in all the will of God, mature and fully assured. (Col 4:12)

Questions

1. How would you describe your prayer life?

2. What is something you can do to improve your prayer life?

3. Who has modeled a devout prayer life for you?

Prayer

I am grateful for those who model devout prayer lives. Thank you for books and resources that challenge and help me. May I continue to grow in my communication with you in all aspects of prayer. May I adore you more. Confess my sin often. Intercede for others faithfully. Be thankful continually. Amen.

57
Ripples

Don and I visited the Billy Graham Library a few years ago and came across a plaque that tracked ripples. Edward Kimball led Moody to Jesus. God used Moody in the life of F. B. Meyer who in turn led Wilber Chapman to the Lord. Wilbur worked with Billy Sunday who invited Mordecai Ham to speak where Billy Graham came to know Jesus. Then, of course God used Mr. Graham to share the gospel with many people around the world. It is fascinating to see what happened because of one Sunday School teacher talking to a shoe clerk about Jesus! Investing in people who invest in other people who invest in other people … God ordains the most amazing ripple effects from the smallest acts of obedience. I am certain that Edward Kimball did not know the impact this one act of obedience of sharing the gospel would have. He was simply being faithful to what God called him to do one day at a time.

I saw a picture of a fountain with individual drips of water dropping into the pooled water below. Each small drop affected the water as the ripples expanded further and further. The symbolism is beautiful!

Sometimes we may be aware when God uses us to cause ripples. We might be talking with a friend, instructing a child, or performing an act of kindness and a person says thank you or somehow lets you know that God used you to change them. They then take what they learned from you and God uses them to touch other lives. Those lives touch other lives. Ripple effect in action. Even when seeing evidence of a ripple, we can't know in this lifetime how far the ripples go.

Most times, however, we don't even recognize when God is using us to make ripples! I've heard that ripple effects are often unintentional. Maybe because of small beginnings or the time it takes to trace the outcomes, people often live and die without knowing the full extent of the influence their lives had on others.

Part of the fascination of ripple effects is that we are unaware of what word or action may start one. It would most likely be something little that one wouldn't think would spark a wildfire. When William Carey went to India, he wasn't thinking about becoming the "father of modern missions." He was simply being obedient to God's call on his life. When Hudson Taylor went to China, his goal wasn't to start the China Inland Mission, but to share the gospel with people there. There are other famous names to whom ripple effects can be traced.

There are many, many more unfamous people whom God has used to create ripple effects to accomplish his purposes around the world. Pastors, missionaries, teachers, doctors, construction workers, carpenters, nurses, homemakers, college students, teenagers, musicians, electricians, and plumbers—it isn't a person's profession that causes ripple effects. It is trusting in Jesus and obeying God in what he has called us to do.

Often, we look at our actions and determine if what we did was valuable based on immediate reactions and results. We have our idea of what success looks like. If it doesn't appear that our ministry is prospering right away, then we might think we've failed or made a mistake. We may be tempted to give up or stop trying. We may grow discouraged and wane in our obedience to the Lord.

We forget about ripples. We overlook the Almighty One who can take one act of obedience or one step of faith and create a ripple effect for generations to come!

Ripples.

Scripture

> Let us not become weary in doing good, for at the proper time we will reap a harvest if we do not give up. Therefore, as we have opportunity, let us do good to all people, especially to those who belong to the family of believers. (Gal 6:9–10)

Questions

1. How have you seen ripples caused by someone you know?

2. How far back can you trace those involved in your story of salvation?

3. How does the idea of ripple effects encourage you today?

Prayer

When disappointed with results, I have often been thankful that this isn't the end of the story. I don't know how you will use what I do today to influence people tomorrow. What looks like failure may be the next step in someone else's story. May I live faithfully and trust you with results. Amen.

58
An Unforgettable Date

When Don and I were in India, we began reading a book called *Forty Unforgettable Dates with Your Mate*.[1] There are chapters for husbands and wives to read separately with ideas for dates and topics to talk about on those dates.

Don read chapter 1. As a result, he took me for lunch at a lovely hotel and had questions he asked me to draw out how I was feeling about life and relationships. He listened actively while we both enjoyed a tasty buffet meal. Afterwards we went shopping to purchase something to remember the day. We bought a tablecloth for our dining room table. Once we purchased it, we saw on the label it was really a bed sheet. But it was our tablecloth and worked perfectly.

I read the next chapter. It was my turn to treat him to a special date. As I thought through the ideas, I got excited. Don loves photography and nature. I wanted to encourage him in that and give him the gift of exploring God's creation. So, I went online and discovered there were some "spectacular" waterfalls that google maps said were about two hours away from where we lived. I couldn't pronounce the name, but it would be a great day trip. I contacted a travel agent who arranged a car and driver. I didn't tell Don where we were going. He was going to be so surprised!

I packed a picnic lunch and could just imagine us sitting by the waterfalls enjoying nature, talking together, and Don taking some amazing pictures of God's beautiful world. The car arrived in the morning. We got in and began our trip.

One hour passed. Two hours passed. We stopped for coffee. Three hours passed. I was so confused. It wasn't supposed to take this long! We should have been there by now. Four hours passed. Five hours passed. The roads were not in good condition. Traffic was crazy at times with other motorcycles, bicycles, cars, trucks, and animals.

---

1 Gary and Barbara Rosberg, *40 Unforgettable Dates with Your Mate* (Carol Stream: Tyndale, 2002).

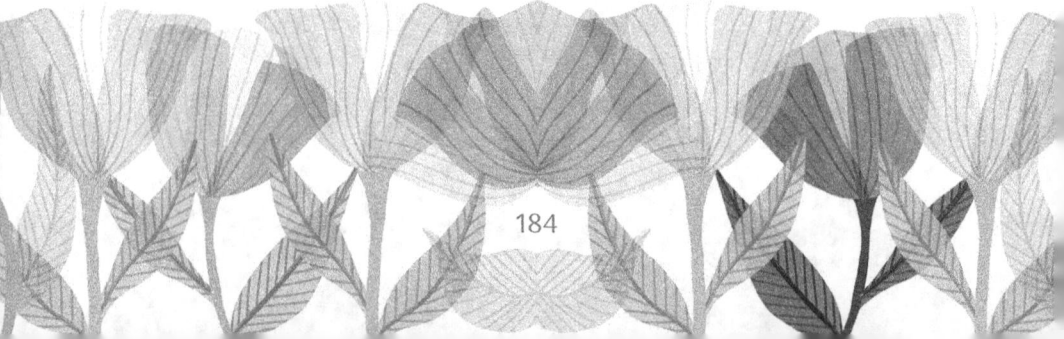

The driver, who said he knew where we were going, kept stopping to ask for directions. We finally arrived at the waterfalls. It was obvious that many others had the same idea I had. There were people everywhere. There was nowhere to have a picnic.

We spent twenty minutes walking and taking pictures. That was ten minutes more than necessary. We got back into the car to begin the five-hour trip back home. About halfway there, I tried to put a positive spin on the hot weather, long drive, bumpy roads, crowded location, gnawing hunger, and all the unexpected events of the day by saying, "It really hasn't been that bad, has it?"

To which Don gently replied, "I'm trying to think of a nice way to say how awful this has been." However, I have often reminded him that the title of the book included the words "unforgettable dates" and that accurately describes our trip to the waterfalls. He can't forget it, no matter how hard he tried!

And just in case he does forget … I have a picture to remind him!

Scripture

You know when I sit and when I rise;
> you perceive my thoughts from afar.

You discern my going out and my lying down;
> you are familiar with all my ways.

Before a word is on my tongue
> you, LORD, know it completely.

You hem me in behind and before,
> and you lay your hand upon me.

Such knowledge is too wonderful for me,
> too lofty for me to attain. (Ps 139:2–6)

Questions

1. How do you normally respond to the unexpected?

2. What role does faith play when we encounter something unforeseen?

3. What is comforting about God always knowing what we don't?

Prayer

You always know what is next. There are no surprises or mysteries for you. When I stumble into the unknown, I am so thankful you are with me and know what will happen. Some surprises I encounter are fun, others are scary. But knowing you know makes all the difference. Amen.

59
Uni-Tasking

Though many years have passed, I still remember the day as a mother of four little children when I multi-tasked to the best of my ability. My baby daughter was hungry, I had to go to the bathroom, and as always there was laundry to do. So, while sitting on the toilet I was also nursing my daughter, and since the washing machine was situated next to the toilet, I began pulling out the damp clothes that eventually needed to be hung outside to dry. I felt harried. In the midst of multi-tasking there was no cuddling my daughter (it was not the most comfortable nursing experience for me or her as my arm swung to and from the washing machine!) nor was there a tender moment gazing into her lovely, big brown eyes. I was thinking of the tasks that needed to be done and I was getting three done at one time!

When the kids were little, life was busy; days were full; nights could be sleepless. Nothing prevented the accumulation of things that needed to be done. I'm sure this is true for moms whether you work across cultures or not; but I think all would agree that stress multiplies when living outside of your home country. There was the soaking of fruits and vegetables in bleach water, boiling drinking water—and not confusing the two! We hung clothes out to dry and thus there was a need for ironing.

Dust from the Sahara blew daily through open windows on hot sunny days which resulted in more housework as well as warm sweaty bodies dirtying their clothes that caused more soiled laundry and the cycle kept repeating! Add to that time with neighbors and friends, helping the kids with homework, play time, family devotions, and settling sibling squabbles as well as marital disagreements. I was tired. I needed to multi-task to survive.

And yet in the hustle and bustle of life, there are other precious moments that stand out to me when it didn't look like a lot was getting done, but my soul was being restored in simply enjoying one thing at a time.

I remember sitting in the one corner of our hot apartment where I could feel a cross breeze and feed my baby. It was quiet. I was still. It was her and me. I could rest and take that time to enjoy the closeness of just my daughter and me. No laundry. No dusting. Just me, her, and a gentle breeze.

During the winters, I set my alarm a little early so that when I got up the apartment was quiet. I put on the tea kettle, lit the oven, sat down by its open door, and read from the Bible. I prayed. Oswald Chambers became a friend as I often read *My Utmost for His Highest*. I sought my heavenly Father in the stillness before doors slammed and feet ran. I didn't appear productively busy, but I met God there, and he prepared me for the day.

I remember a few late-night talks at the foot of our kids' beds. I knew there were other things I needed to do. I was tired, but on those occasions when I took the time to sit, I heard deeper questions and enjoyed unrushed conversations with four of the most important people in the world to me. Those other things to do would be there later and would be there again next week and next month and next year. There would always be tasks. There will always be laundry. Not so, these opportunities when my kids were living at home.

In today's world, it is way more difficult to concentrate on one task at a time. Our phones are dinging, social media beckons, computers are waiting—all urgently trying to divert our attention away from the important people directly in front of us. We now mentally and physically multi-task more than ever. It can seem more of a priority to connect with people around the world than the ones in our living room!

When I'm with my grandchildren, twelve of the most significant people in my world that I don't get to see very often, I am sad to say there is sometimes a smart phone in my hand and multi-tasking on my mind. Once, before I knew it, I had missed an opportunity to interact face to face with my full attention on a little person who might not recognize by my actions that they are more important to me than anything on my phone.

Spending time with God away from my smart phone, sitting to read a book that encourages my soul, resting on a Sunday afternoon, chatting with a friend over a cup of coffee ignoring even the slighted buzz of my pocketed phone, actively listening to my grandson's imaginative story without interruptions—these uni-task opportunities are intentionally delightful and ultimately more purposeful than doing even a thousand things at once!

Life shouldn't be so focused on being *productive* that I lose sight of living *purposefully*.

We have one life—each day is an opportunity in which to choose intentionally and meaningfully to live with purpose. There is a time for productive multi-tasking. We must also make time for purposeful uni-tasking!

Scripture

> For no one can lay any foundation other than the one already laid, which is Jesus Christ. If anyone builds on this foundation using gold, silver, costly stones, wood, hay or straw, their work will be shown for what it is, because the Day will bring it to light. It will be revealed with fire, and the fire will test the quality of each person's work. If what has been built survives, the builder will receive a reward. If it is burned up, the builder will suffer loss but yet will be saved—even though only as one escaping through the flames. (1 Cor 3:11–15)

Questions

1. What are the downsides and upsides of multi-tasking?

2. How can you live more intentionally in your relationships by multi-tasking less?

3. What would you consider your top priorities?

Prayer

I have only so many hours in a day. My energy is limited. May I choose wisely how I invest my time and energy. May I honor you in my relationships by how I esteem those around me. May my attention not wander from the present and who is in front of me at any given moment. Amen.

60

Hellos, Goodbyes, and Ugly Cries

There are many things I don't like. Cold showers. Lukewarm tea. Liver and onions. Pillows that are too high. Tires that are too low. Cockroaches. But at the top of the list is saying goodbye.

As I write this, I am sitting in a hotel room and my flight home is in the morning. I just finished having an ugly cry. You know what I mean, right? It's the kind of cry you can't hold in any longer—it bursts out in slightly hysterical sobbing noises. It is like my heart has broken open and its fluid's only outflow is in the tears running down my cheeks.

No one has died. Nothing is devastating. So, I feel like a whiner. Guilt creeps its way into my heart for feeling this sad at saying goodbye. I know I am blessed to be able to say hello. But sadness feels overwhelming at this moment.

I was with my daughter and her family for about two weeks helping after the birth of their third child. I washed dishes, read stories, played hide and seek, did laundry, talked, and listened. Changing diapers became normal again. I rocked, patted, and kissed all the littles multiple times daily. I enjoyed chatting with my daughter and my son-in-law. The time went quickly, though, and the day came to say goodbye.

I was brave as I hugged and kissed my daughter and each of her three children goodbye. Hugs and kisses were generously given by the four-year-old and two-year-old. I pecked the baby's cheek and said a quick goodbye. Avoiding long goodbyes is necessary for me to avoid becoming a blubbering mess. I kept a tight rein on my emotions as my son-in-law drove me to the airport. Hugging him goodbye, I kept up a strong front. At the check-in counter my eyes filled but didn't spill. I stood stoically through the immigration line. I kept the tears at bay on the plane. All the way to the hotel, I chatted with different people. No one could tell I was one huge tear drop on the inside waiting to escape.

Alone in my room, self-control abandoned me. Tears flowed.

Goodbyes are a big part of this life to which God has called us. I have lost count of how many hellos and goodbyes we have said through the years. Family members, team members, friends—all coming and going, never seeing some again in this lifetime. Other times we have surprise reunions, but always say goodbye again. It doesn't get any easier. There are more and more loved people to whom we say goodbye.

I wonder if one reason goodbyes are so hard is that our souls weren't originally made to say them. This is true when we encounter death. We are eternal creatures, made to live forever in God's presence. But because of sin, death entered the picture. Our bodies break down. Goodbyes happen when hearts stop beating … for those in Christ the goodbye is only temporary, but the grief often feels like it will last forever.

I don't know if that reasoning counts when families just live far apart. Maybe we all wouldn't have stayed in the garden of Eden if sin hadn't entered the world. There might have been worlds to explore and other gardens to cultivate. Families would have said goodbye to each other then, too.

It can be easy for me to focus so much on the sorrow of saying goodbye that I lose sight of the joy in the many hellos. But hellos don't take away the sadness of goodbyes. After time together, I miss my family even more keenly. But it is worth the pain of saying goodbye to experience the joy of saying hello. It is worth the heartbreak to treasure heartfelt moments. Goodbyes enable me to savor the preciousness of hellos more fully.

I wonder why "good" is even part of goodbye. Merriam Webster says that "goodbye" is an alteration of "God be with you" (circa 1580). That phrase comforts me. I know God is with each of us all the time. God never leaves so he never has to say goodbye! The goodbyes I said today could remind me of a day that is coming when we will say a final goodbye to all goodbyes!

However, until that day I will delight in the hellos and take comfort that when I say goodbye, God doesn't. He soothes our souls, especially during ugly cries. God is with us.

Scripture

Remember your word to your servant,
    for you have given me hope.
My comfort in my suffering is this:
    Your promise preserves my life. (Ps 119:49–50)

Questions

1. What caused your most recent "ugly cry"?

2. How have you experienced God's comfort in all your goodbyes?

3. What role does an eternal perspective play in our need for comfort?

Prayer

One of the names of your Holy Spirit in my old King James Bible is Comforter. I am thankful for your comfort. I am thankful for the truth of Scripture that soothes my soul when it is troubled. I am thankful that one day all tears will be wiped away and there will be no more sadness and no more goodbyes. Thank you for hope amid sorrows here. Amen.

61
Saying Goodbye as the One Who Stays

I stood in the driveway waving as my daughter and her family drove away. They were on their way to the airport to return overseas, and I was still in the US. This is one of my first goodbyes as a stayer.

They were packing. I had unpacked. They were sorting, finding room to take back all they needed. The sounds and processes were familiar. I had lots of practice with packing and choosing what goes with me and what doesn't. I knew how to do that. But I realized that I hadn't had much practice watching others prepare to leave. I was normally the one packing my suitcase. I was the one in a car on the way to the airport.

I felt odd. I thought, "So, this is what it is like to stay and say goodbye to your loved ones who leave."

The emotions are not the same. For those leaving, though sad, they anticipate what is next. What will God do? How will he be at work? Staying behind felt more about the present. A return to normal, not enthusiastically looking ahead. It reminded me of when my parents said goodbye to us as we left for our first term overseas.

We were standing in the driveway with our three young children saying goodbye to my parents. We said a tearful goodbye, knowing it would be a long time before we saw each other again. We were heading off to another corner of the world where the unknown awaited us. My heart was hurting, yet I also felt a flutter of excitement at what life held. At the time, I didn't wonder how they felt returning home.

Coming and going. I've said many goodbyes through the years, but now I am the one staying while saying goodbye. My daughter and her family were off and running. I stand in the driveway, wave, and walk slowly back to the house. It feels empty and quiet.

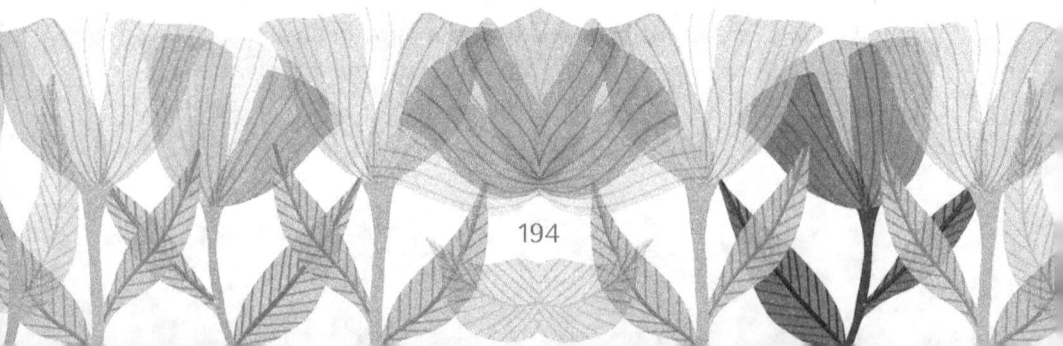

Saying Goodbye as the One Who Stays

I realize anew how different it is for the one going from the one staying. Goodbyes are hard both ways, but I think it is harder for the stayer. I never would have imagined that. For the leavers there is the pain of goodbye, which is difficult. But the pain mixes with the anticipation of what is next. The stayer knows what is next. Anticipation is missing.

As my daughter traveled, she texted progress reports. She made it to London. I remember flying through London, looking for a quiet place to sit, waiting for my next flight. Through her, I vicariously made the trip. But when her trip was over, I was still in the same place.

But it is a good place. A new home where roots can deepen and ministry can still thrive. As I settle I even sense anticipation building. It feels a bit different from the anticipation when leaving, but I am expectant of what God will do in me and in this new place as I stay.

Expectancy. Anticipation. Hope. None of these depend on a certain location or whether we are the ones who stay or go. We have hope because we trust in the God of hope who guides our steps. He is with me here and has a plan. I can't wait to see how it unfolds!

Scripture

When Paul had finished speaking, he knelt down with all of them and prayed. They all wept as they embraced him and kissed him. What grieved them most was his statement that they would never see his face again. Then they accompanied him to the ship. (Acts 20:36–38)

Questions

1. How do you say goodbye well?

2. How would you compare the goodbyes of the one who goes and the one who stays?

3. What would help comfort those who have recently said a hard goodbye?

Prayer

One day there will be no more goodbyes. But until then, we have them all the time. The more we love someone, the harder the goodbye is. Final goodbyes are especially hard. Help me remember that for those who know you, it is temporary. Thank you for the hope we have of an eternity at home with you and no more goodbyes. Amen.

Acknowledgments

I am thankful to God who doesn't discard clay pots but chooses to empower and use them for his glory.

I am grateful for my husband. His adventurous, obedient heart led me on journeys of faith I never would have attempted on my own.

I thank God for my children and grandchildren who work to stay connected to us wherever we have lived.

I appreciate our prayer and financial supporters who have loved us and prayed for us throughout our ministry. For over thirty-eight years they have partnered with us, spurring us on with generosity, grace, and kindness.

visit us at missionbooks.org

Screams in the Desert: Hope and Humor for Women in Cross-Cultural Ministry
Sue Eenigenburg

Screams in the Desert is an invitation to participate in one woman's cross-cultural journey and the lessons she learns along the way. Join Sue for trips to the zoo, bouts of illness, landmine fields, miscommunications, and other everyday experiences of life in a foreign country. Providing women with examples to learn by, Scripture to meditate on, and space to write about personal experiences, *Screams in the Desert* offers hope and humor to women working cross-culturally.

More Screams, Different Deserts: Joy and Perseverance for Women in Cross-Cultural Ministry
Sue Eenigenburg

More Screams, Different Deserts is another invitation to join Sue on her adventures in cross-cultural living and biblical studies that have helped her along the way. With years of experience in cross-cultural ministry, Sue realizes that joy and perseverance are essential for thriving in life and ministry. Her stories and insights encourage women to look to Jesus, our only hope wherever we live. Questions and resources at the end of each chapter will help readers think through personal application and find additional help.

Grit to Stay Grace to Go: Staying Well in Cross-Cultural Ministry
Sue Eenigenburg and Eva Burkholder

Grit to Stay Grace to Go normalizes the challenges of ministry through honest and humorous stories from the authors' own lives as well as testimonies from many other workers. The point is to help cross-cultural workers not just to stay, but to stay well, by countering lies with truth. This workbook provides thoughtful reflection questions, practical action steps, and suggested prayers. It encourages stayers to process their grief, guilt, and relief when saying goodbye to goers. In this way, they can move forward with forgiveness and humility and truly bless the departing ones.

Expectations and Burnout: Women Surviving the Great Commission
Sue Eenigenburg and Robynn Bliss

Missionary women have high expectations when they respond to God's call; of themselves, their mission agencies, host cultures, churches, co-workers, and even of God. These expectations are often times impossible to fulfill and can lead to mental and physical exhaustion. In this book, Sue provides research and surveys from the field while Robynn lends her own personal experiences to demonstrate how burnout can happen and how God can bring life from ashes. Join them as they explore how to develop realistic expectations and yet maintain faith in our sovereign God.

When the Serving Gets Tough: A Thirty-Day Devotional for Missionaries
Carol B. Ghattas

Many who answer the call to serve among the nations will, at some point, hit a brick wall in their faith. In *When Serving Gets Tough*, veteran missionary and author Carol Ghattas shares her experiences, providing practical guidance and hope through Scripture. Each daily entry is designed to help missionaries reconnect with their faith, find strength in God's promises, and press on in their calling despite difficulties. Ghattas acknowledges that there is no one-size-fits-all solution to ministry trials but emphasizes that there is one God always ready to help and heal.

www.ingramcontent.com/pod-product-compliance
Lightning Source LLC
Chambersburg PA
CBHW050223100526
44585CB00017BA/1891